Leasing the Ivory Tower

The Corporate Takeover of Academia

Praise for *Leasing the Ivory Tower*

"This work performs a signal public service. Soley has shown beyond a doubt that not only is the conservative claim that the universities are a hotbed of radical faculty a fantasy, but that this charge conceals an alarming and perilous truth. Higher education, Soley demonstrates, has been transformed into a corporate realm and a new profit center for Big Business."

—Herbert I. Schiller, author of *Culture, Inc.*

"Read it and resist. Soley sounds the alarm: It's time to take back our universities from those who exploit them for personal and corporate gain. *Leasing the Ivory Tower* is necessary ammunition for campus and community activists organizing to make education meet the needs of the public, not the profit seekers."

—Robin Templeton, UNPLUG

"This extensively researched and footnoted work confirms what most student activists already know from daily experience: that the Academy increasingly functions as little more than a publicly subsidized research and develoment arm for the Fortune 500.

"Media frothing about 'political correctness' aside, *Leasing the Ivory Tower* demonstrates conclusively that the truly pervasive influence in American intellectual culture is not 'P.C.' but 'B.C.'—Big Corporations."

—Robert McClure, National Progressive Student Network

"*Leasing the Ivory Tower* deals with the 'political correctness' the corporate community has quietly imposed on academia, which is vastly more important in compromising academic integrity than any challenges from below (which command so much mainstream attention and indignation). Enlightening and well-researched, *Leasing the Ivory Tower* deserves wide attention and should open a much needed debate about the real threats to academic freedom."

—Edward S. Herman, author of *Beyond Hypocrisy*

Leasing the Ivory Tower

The Corporate Takeover of Academia

by Lawrence C. Soley

South End Press

Boston, MA

Cover by Joonhee Lee
Text design and production by the South End Press Collective
Printed in the U.S.A.

Library of Congress Cataloguing-in-Publication Data
    Soley, Lawrence C.
    Leasing the ivory tower: the corporate takeover of academia/
by Lawrence C. Soley.
        p. cm.
    Includes bibliographical references and index.
    ISBN 0-89608-504-X : $40.00. — ISBN 0-89608-503-1 (pbk.) :
$13.00
        1. Endowments—United States. 2. Endowment of research—
United States. 3. Corporations—Charitable contributions—
United States. 4. Intellectual cooperation. 5. Academic
freedom—United States. I. Title.
    LB2336.S66   1995
    378'.02—dc20   94-39872
                           CIP

South End Press, 116 Saint Botolph Street, Boston, MA 02115
    01 00 99 98 97 96 95   1 2 3 4 5 6 7 8 9

® GCIU

Contents

Preface

By Leonard Minsky
National Coalition for Universities in the Public Interest

Not a month goes by without tales of fraud and misconduct in university research labs, student demonstrations against rising tuitions, cutbacks in academic programs, and congressional inquiries into bogus and fly-by-night colleges. As Professor Soley demonstrates in the following pages, fraud, deception, and corporate corruption in U.S. universities have become commonplace.

Leasing the Ivory Tower exposes the many facets of the corporate takeover of the university. From the revolving door between corporate CEOs and university administrators, to foundation "fronts" set up by corporations to fund "objective" research, to the corporate R&D in university labs, corporate influence in academia has profoundly transformed higher education.

However, just as with many other problems in this country—declining incomes, rising crime, and growing ineptitude in Washington—corporate obfuscation and an uncritical media make it difficult to see the overall picture, and the agents and agencies responsible.

The corporate assault on universities has been part of a deliberate corporate campaign to reintroduce power onto campuses, after the activism of the 1960s had largely discredited corporate sponsorship. With science and technology-oriented industries perceived as the wave of the future, corporations were eager to exploit the heavy federal investment in university-based research.

Universities could offer many benefits to industries seeking a better bottom line. Corporations could sponsor and direct taxpayer-funded university research, without making the terms of the university-corporate contracts public. They could avoid the sting of risky investments in new research, because the public was paying the real costs of research and development through federal grants to universities. They could reduce their taxes with their small, tax-free investments in university research.

At the time, the failure of American industry to develop new technologies had been a major cause of economic recession. Corporations, in their bid for access to university resources, argued that the need for "competitiveness" was a national emergency: the vast public investment in university research and development was wasted if it didn't benefit industry more directly, by producing new high-tech products.

At the same time, President Reagan promoted his Star Wars research program, demanding agreement to continue the research from a scientific community skeptical of the technical, scientific, and political goals of the program. Scientists were specifically threatened with the loss of their grant money if they openly opposed the program, and the re-introduction of corporate-sponsored research subjected university researchers to a double whammy of corporate and military chauvinism. Ultimately, several pieces of legislation enacted in the 1980s, including the University and Small Business Patent Procedures Act of 1980, acted as leverage for the corporatization of university-based research.

In the 1990s, corporate influence in universities has continued unchecked, obscured by the phony "political correctness" (PC) wars. According to pro-corporate rhetoric, the university has been colonized—not by corporations, but by liberals and minority groups intent on servicing a narrow ideology. During the 1980s, a generation of successful women's, civil rights, and environmental struggles had landed a significant commitment of financial resources for women's studies, African-American studies, and environmental studies programs at universities. Environmentalists supported by university positions revised science curricula to reflect environmental concerns, acted as expert witnesses against polluting companies, and won significant settlements in whistleblower-inspired lawsuits. These, and other liberal campaigns, were perceived as an obstacle to renewed corporate control. Conservative and pro-corporate critics who have targeted liberals and minority groups in their PC attacks have been motivated, in the main, not by the perception of a threat to free inquiry but by the bottom line.

As *Leasing the Ivory Tower* demonstrates, universities have been the eager partners and co-participants in industry's interventions on campus. Universities, once proud defenders of academic freedom and critical thought, are now ever more exclusively the cradle of industrial invention. Corporations steal the intellectual property of students and faculty, while universities resell this property at below market rates through exclusive licensing agreements. The costs to the public are manifold: for one, corporations can shield new products, especially drugs and biomedical devices, from critical review.

The past role of universities to serve the public has been hopelessly compromised. The cynical role now played by corporatized universities has made them untrustworthy arbiters of the public good. *Leasing the Ivory Tower*'s detailed account of corporatism in higher education should serve as a wake-up call to faculty, students, and alumni: a coordinated effort is needed to thwart the systematic selling out of higher education.

—Leonard Minsky
Washington, D.C.
April 1995

Chapter One

Underneath the Ivy

Books such as *Illiberal Education* by Dinesh D'Souza and *Tenured Radicals* by Roger Kimball have sent the media on a snipe hunt for "political correctness." Political correctness (PC) is a phrase popularized by political conservatives to describe an array of academic trends—including feminist scholarship, multiculturalism, new literary theories such as deconstructionism, and even hate speech restrictions—that conservatives find objectionable. However, rather than describing what actually happened on college campuses during the 1980s and 1990s—the takeover of universities by corporations, tycoons, and foundations—these books, with the support of uncritical media, assert that '60s radicals have seized the administration of universities just as they seized administration buildings two decades earlier.

"Traditionally liberal professors are retiring and making way for a new generation weaned on the assorted ideologies of the late 1960s, such as the movement for black separatism and the burgeoning causes of feminism and gay rights," D'Souza writes. "Already their influence is in many places dominant."[1] In *Tenured Radicals*, Roger Kimball writes in a similar vein, "Yesterday's student radical is today's tenured professor or academic dean...It is important to appreciate the extent to which the radical vision of the sixties has not so much been abandoned as internalized by many who came of age then and who now teach at and administer our institutions of higher education."[2]

Stephen Balch, president of the pompously named National Association of Scholars, the nation's leading PC-bashing group, has also sounded the alarm against left-wing academic dominance. He warns that during "the 60's an exceptionally large cohort of university students were [sic] absorbed into the political culture of the Left and the enthusiasms that it spawned. Many of them chose to make careers for themselves in higher education...This academic generation, now entering full professional maturity, is gaining a considerable hand in the governance of departments, programs, and whole institutions."[3]

Newsweek, New York, Time, and other magazines and newspapers have blindly repeated the assertions of critics such as Balch, Kimball, and D'Souza. *Newsweek* asserted that political correctness is "the program of a generation of campus radicals who grew up in the '60s and are now achieving positions of academic influence."[4] Having taken control of universities, these radicals have allegedly unleashed a Red terror that includes restrictions on free speech, ideological conformity, and the harassment of professors who speak out against the terror. *New York* magazine claims that "the supreme irony of the new fundamentalism is that the generation that produced the free-speech movement in Berkeley...is now trying to restrict speech and control the behavior of a new generation of students."[5]

The proof of this radical takeover consists of a few tales that are endlessly retold. The media have repeated the same stories so often that University of Illinois dean James Carey speculated that they were obtained from "a central anecdote bank at some conservative Washington think tank accessible through an 800—no make that a 900—number."[6] For example, one of the most often-mentioned incidents of political correctness occurred at the University of Pennsylvania. Roger Kimball described the incident in the *Gannett Center Journal*, which is published at Columbia University in New York City by an on-campus research center funded by Al Neuharth, the former Gannett Corporation CEO. Kimball wrote that "at the University of Pennsylvania, a student on a panel for 'diversity education' wrote a memorandum to her colleagues in which she expressed her 'deep regard for the individual and...desire to protect the freedom of all members of society.' A university administrator responded by circling the passage just quoted, underlining the word 'individual,' and commenting, 'This is a "RED FLAG" phrase today, which is considered by many to be RACIST. Arguments that champion the individual over the group ultimately privileges [sic] the "individuals" belonging to the largest or dominant group.'"[7] This incident was one of several mentioned in a *New York* magazine cover story, and D'Souza and Kimball describe the same incident almost verbatim in their books. The *Chicago Tribune* and other publications have also publicized it.[8]

Another frequently retold story concerns Harvard University professor Stephan Thernstrom, who was allegedly accused of racial insensitivity for using the word "Indians" instead of "Native Americans" and the word "Oriental, with its imperialist overtones," when describing an Asian religion. Thernstrom was also accused of insensitivity for his discussions of the Black family, according to several widely repeated, but somewhat variant, descriptions of the incident. The Thernstrom case is discussed in D'Souza's book, *The New Republic*, *The New York Review of Books*, *New York*, "This Week With David Brinkley," and even the British *Independent*. The incident is also mentioned in Martin Anderson's *Impostors in the Temple* and Thomas Sowell's *Inside American Education*.[9]

Not only have a few tales been often retold, but some of these tales appear to be more fabrication than fact. According to *Newsday* and *Mother Jones*, an incident described in the *Wall Street Journal*, *New York Post*, and the *Binghamton Press & Sun Bulletin* contained more embellishments than substance. The articles described events that supposedly occurred at the State University of New York at Binghamton (SUNY). As the *Journal* reported the incident: "Two hundred students—some carrying canes and sticks—come pouring into a quiet lecture hall and post themselves menacingly in the aisles and at the exits. The threat of violence is clear and soon fulfilled. The mob disrupts the talk, jeers the speaker. An elderly, distinguished professor in the audience barely escapes a beating at the hands of one of this mob...[which] has come to wreck the proceedings because the talk was given under the auspices of the university's newly formed chapter of the National Association of Scholars, an organization leading the struggle to preserve academic freedom, currently under siege in our universities."[10]

The journalist who penned this account didn't attend the SUNY forum. However, the description matches one in a memo sent to SUNY president Lois Defleur by Professor Michael Mittelstadt, a National Association of Scholars member. Mittelstadt also called the local television station, complaining that its newscast had low-keyed rather than played up a disruptive incident at the forum, *Mother Jones*'s David Beers discovered.

According to witnesses, including a television reporter and an on-campus plainclothes police officer, the newspaper accounts were mostly hyperbole. One student disrupted the forum, but the audience prevented him from continuing his disruptive activities. The disruptive student was later disciplined by the university for his actions. "No one was hurt, no property was destroyed, the entire lecture was delivered, the question and answer session was spirited, but civil," *Mother Jones* reported. The sticks and canes described in the news reports consisted of "one walking cane used as such, and a handful of pledge canes carried as symbols of fraternity membership." None were brandished during the forum.[11] *Newsday* also reported that just one student disrupted the presentations, and that the disruption lasted just four minutes. With that exception, the speeches were delivered without incident.[12]

Along with hyperbole and repetition, PC-bashers' arguments are also riddled with inconsistencies. These critics, who claim that college campuses are now run by radical feminists, African-American nationalists, and other political dissidents, can't explain why women, African Americans, and other peoples of color are underrepresented as faculty—and underpaid—in comparison with their white, male counterparts. African Americans and women comprise a far smaller percentage of the faculty than of the student population in universities, and they hold an even smaller percentage of administrative positions. For example, a study of women's employment at the University of Wisconsin at Madison, a university that has frequently been described by rightists as a bastion of political correctness, found that women held 20 percent of the faculty postions, but just 11 percent of dean positions and 13 percent of department chair positions.[13]

Moreover, women are paid less than their male counterparts. According to the U.S. government, male assistant professors received an average salary of $36,969 in 1991-92, whereas female assistant professors received an average salary of $34,063. At the full professor rank, men were paid $58,494, but women were paid $51,621.[14] If feminists were indeed running universities, it's safe to assume that this pay discrepancy would not exist.

The Corporate Roots

Not surprisingly, the outspoken critics of political correctness have been silent about the politicizing of campuses by right-wing foundations, corporations, and tycoons. They have also had nothing to say about free-speech restrictions at numerous universities (particularly those with religious affiliations) where liberal professors have been silenced. For example, neither *Illiberal Education* nor *Tenured Radicals* mentions the case of Rev. Charles Curran, who was removed from his tenured teaching post at the Catholic University of America in 1987 because of his liberal views on abortion, divorce, homosexuality, premarital sex, and contraception.[15]

Taking their cues from conservative critics, the media have also dwelled almost exclusively on a few stories about PC, and in so doing have missed the real story about academe. The *real* story is about university physics and electrical engineering departments being seduced by Pentagon contracts; molecular biology, biochemistry, and medicine departments being wooed by drug companies and biotech firms; and university computer science departments being in bed with Big Blue and a few high-tech chip makers. The story about universities in the 1980s and 1990s is that they will turn a trick for anybody with money to invest; and the only ones with money are corporations, millionaires, and foundations. These investments in universities have dramatically changed the mission of higher education; they have led universities to attend to the interests of their well-heeled patrons, rather than those of students.

Many of the PC-bashing critics receive money from the same corporations and foundations abetted by their obfuscating analyses. For example, D'Souza is a "scholar" at a conservative, Washington-based think tank, the American Enterprise Institute, which is funded by many of the same tycoons, corporations, and foundations that have invested heavily in universities during the past decade. Kimball, in addition to being a fiction writer, is editor of the conservative magazine *New Criterion*, which receives grants from well-funded trusts like the John M. Olin Foundation, a nonprofit corporation endowed by a former munitions manufacturer. The Olin Foundation has also invested heavily in universities during the past decade. It funds programs of study that promote politically conservative solutions to legal and social problems at Stanford University in Palo Alto, California, Georgetown University in Washington, D.C., and numerous other universities.

Stephan Balch's group is also funded by some of the same tycoons and foundations that poured money into universities. For example, the Sarah Scaife Foundation gave the National Association of Scholars hundreds of thousands of dollars between 1988 and 1992. The Scaife Foundation also bankrolled conservative "research" centers that operate on the campuses of Smith College in Northampton, Massachusetts; Clemson University in Clemson, South Carolina; Boston University; Stanford; and the University of Chicago. Similarly, Martin Anderson and Thomas Sowell are "scholars" at Stanford's Hoover Institution, which received funds from many of the same corporations, foundations, and conservative fat cats that underwrite the American Enterprise Institute and the National Association of Scholars.

The University of California at Los Angeles (UCLA) typifies in many ways what has happened to universities in the real world outside anti-PC rhetoric. Corporations have contracted with the university for research, hired its professors as consultants, and endowed professorships. Foundations have established independently operating fiefdoms on the UCLA campus, and tycoons have become the advisers and namesakes of departments.[16] Moreover, several other universities have gone further than just naming professorships and departments after millionaires and corporations, as UCLA has. For example, Glassboro State College in Glassboro, New Jersey changed its name to Rowan College after receiving $100 million from industrialist Henry M. Rowan, the founder of a furnace company. Not since the Stalin era in the Soviet Union has a living individual had a monument of this size named after him.

When donations are made to higher education by corporations, the donors often receive massive benefits, even when strings aren't attached. In addition to tax writeoffs, corporations get enormous public relations benefits from their donations. Philip Morris's Miller Brewing Company, for example, donates $150,000 annually to the Thurgood Marshall Scholarship Fund, which provides scholarships to African-American students. But Miller also spends more than $300,000 a year to advertise the program and its contributions, and these advertisements carry the Miller logo. The corporation has also purchased time at professional basketball games to tout its donation.[17]

University administrators claim that such corporate and foundation money is accepted without strings. But this claim doesn't mean that universities are independent of their benefactors, according to Cal Bradford, a former fellow at the University of Minnesota's Humphrey Institute for Public Policy. Bradford should know. His contract wasn't extended after he criticized the university's ties to corporations. The outside funds "determine what universities will teach and research, what direction the university will take," Bradford says. "If universities would decide that they need an endowed chair in English, and then try to raise the money for it, it would be one thing. But that's not what happens. Corporate donors decide to fund chairs in areas that they want research done. Their decisions decide which topics universities explore and which aren't."[18]

In some cases, the influence of donors is direct rather than subtle:

*At the University of Nevada at Las Vegas, the College of Hotel Administration negotiated a $2 million "gift" from the Japanese-owned ACE Denken Company, which manufactures slot machines. The arrangement ties the college to ACE Denken in perpetuity, pending a review every five years. The $2 million donation endowed a doctoral program in hotel administration. For the gift, university administrators promised to publish an annual monograph named for ACE on "issues facing the casino and gaming industry," to sponsor an annual seminar for ACE management and their friends on a topic picked by ACE, and to present ACE with an annual report on developments in gambling technology. The board of regents of the university initially rejected the deal, calling it a contract, not a gift. After some negotiations, however, they agreed to the deal with a few weak restrictions.[19]

*The $100 million gift to Glassboro State College from Henry M. Rowan in 1992 came with political strings explicitly attached.

One part of the gift consisted of $3 million in scholarships for the children of Rowan's employees. However, the scholarships were only for children of Rowan's nonunion employees. Rowan stated that he would make scholarships available to employees "who have worked harmoniously with their company," not those who "won their contracts through threats and strikes."[20] Glassboro State College officials accepted this discriminatory policy, stating that they didn't "have any problem with an individual giving to defined groups as long as it's not in opposition to the interests of the institution." Union officials denounced the agreement as typical of Rowan's antiunionism.[21] Eventually, pressures from unions, state legislators, and the media, not from the university, forced Rowan to reverse his antiunion stance and allow scholarships to be given to his union employees, too. Despite this reversal, Glassboro State's pronouncement indicates the unprincipled positions that universities are willing to embrace in order to get their hands on corporate and tycoon money.

Glassboro State is not an isolated case. Universities are constantly searching for new funding. One reason university administrators have strongly supported the emphasis on research and other noninstructional projects at their institutions—even at the expense of teaching—is that such projects are perceived to enhance a university's prestige and to have the potential of bringing in large sums of money. Universities are typically classified as to whether they are a "research institution," "liberal arts college," or another class of university.[22] Georgetown, Harvard University in Cambridge, Massachusetts, the Massachusetts Institute of Technology (MIT) also in Cambridge, Stanford, and Yale University in New Haven, Connecticut are classed as research institutions, and most administrators would like to see their universities described as being in the same class as these institutions.

In addition to prestige, research can potentially lead to direct economic benefits. The University and Small Business Patent Procedures Act of 1980 stimulated a race by universities to secure patents on their research discoveries, in the belief that the patents might someday be valuable. Between 1986 and 1989, the number of patents issued to universities doubled from 619 to 1,145.[23] The number of patents that universities secure, rather than the success universities have in educating students, is now used as a measure by which university administrators demonstrate their accomplishments.[24]

Administrators see these patents as a long-run method for generating revenues, but this has so far proved to be an illusion. Universities typically have received little money from the research produced in their laboratories. The nation's biggest royalty recipient among universities is Stanford, which received $13 million in royalty revenues in 1990. This amounts to about 1 percent of Stanford's budget. Most universities received far less in royalties. The University of Pennsylvania, which is classed as a "research institution," received just $750,000 in royalties in 1989, and Penn's royalty revenues were higher that those of most universities.[25]

When universities do get large royalties, they usually come at a very high cost to the public, as Michigan State University's (MSU) cisplatin patent demonstrates. MSU received over $60 million in royalties from Bristol-Myers during the past decade for its patent on cisplatin, an anti-cancer drug used for treating bladder, testicular, and ovarian cancers. Bristol-Myers Squibb received an exclusive license to sell cisplatin (which means that only Bristol-Myers can produce the drug), even though MSU had developed cisplatin with federal funding.[26] Bristol-Myers's profits from the drug have been enormous because it has had a monopoly on production and sales.

When Bristol-Myers's exclusive licensing agreement came up for renewal, a half-dozen drug manufacturers expressed interest in also producing the drug. Some legislators favored ending the exclusivity agreement. However, a consortium of universities and representatives of Bristol-Myers lobbied the National Institutes of Health (NIH), which funded MSU's research, to extend the exclusivity agreement, despite the high prices that Bristol-Myers had been charging cancer victims for the drug. In the end, the NIH sided with the universities and Bristol-Myers, assuring that the drug would remain expensive.[27]

Government actions have promoted these increasing ties between business and universities. Although universities have always pandered to wealthy patrons, universities' toadyism intensified after President Reagan slashed spending on domestic programs. Reagan's cuts to student loans and funding for grant-giving agencies put the pinch on universities. For example, the college work-study program was cut by 26.5 percent, after adjusting for inflation. At the NIH, budget cuts resulted in the funding of just 20 percent of highly meritorious research proposals, as opposed to the 45-55 percent funded before Reagan took office.[28]

When grants to universities from agencies such as the NIH declined, universities began looking to the private sector and well-funded Pentagon programs for money. Today, some academic disciplines have become completely enslaved to corporations and the Pentagon for research dollars. For example, $1.8 billion dollars was allocated to university research by the Defense Department in 1993. "That money accounts for more than 80 percent of all Federal research funds for electrical engineering, more than 70 percent of those for materials and metallurgy, and more than 55 percent of those for computer science," the *New York Times* reported.[29]

Two federal laws—the previously mentioned 1980 University and Small Business Patent Procedures Act (P.L. 96-517), which was supplemented by a 1983 executive order extending the law to large corporations, and the 1981 Recovery Tax Act (P.L. 97-34)—helped cultivate the current relationship between universities and business. The 1980 law and later executive order allowed universities to sell patent rights derived from research to corporations, even if the federal government was the primary funder of the research that led to the patents. The 1981 law increased corporate tax deductions for "donations" made to universities.

These laws have made it worthwhile for corporations to get involved with educational institutions. By sticking some of their dough into universities, corporations are able to buy the results of university research, even though much of the research is funded by the federal government. While federal tax dollars fund about $7 billion worth of research, corporate dollars are used to buy access to the results of the research—at just a fraction of their actual cost. This subsidy to corporations has had a positive impact on corporate bottom lines, particularly in the fields of biotechnology and pharmaceuticals. Corporations have been able to shift part of their research-and-development costs to universities, thereby increasing corporate profits.

The costs of research and other work done at universities, however, are not all picked up by corporate dollars, government grants, or foundation monies. They also come from tuition-paying students, who have been forced to subsidize projects that benefit multinational corporations. High research costs, which arise from the need for expensive, state-of-the-art research laboratories and from reduced teaching loads for faculty researchers, have caused tuition to skyrocket.[30]

At major research universities such as MIT, Harvard, and Stanford, the combined cost of tuition, student fees, and room and board now exceeds $25,000 annually. At public universities, tuition is lower but has been increasing at an even more rapid rate than at private institutions, as state legislatures have reduced their funding for higher education.[31] At public universities, tuition rates increased 170 percent between 1980 and 1992.[32] Increased tuition costs have had the greatest impact on the poor and minorities, particularly African-American men, whose enrollment at universities has decreased rather than increased during the past decade. African-American students comprised 9.8 percent of college enrollment in 1984 but only 9.2 percent in 1992.[33]

While some corporations have contributed to universities to increase their profitability, others, such as the Loctite Corp. and Smith-Kline Beecham, have funded higher education for ideological reasons. The heads of many large companies such as these are dedicated conservatives who want college classrooms to preach the glory of corporate capitalism. For example, William Grala, Smith-Kline's vice president for public affairs, admitted that his company's funding of academic projects was for "the preservation of the system" and to "strengthen democratic capitalism." Smith-Kline's money went to conservative academics who wrote books that provided an "adequate theoretical explanation of democratic capitalism acceptable to the intellectual world," said Grala.[34]

Given the benefits that corporations receive from pouring money into academia, it is little wonder that corporate dollars going to universities increased almost threefold between 1980 and 1986. Businesses spent about $235 million on university-sponsored research in 1980; by 1986, they were spending about $600 million. By 1991, the annual investment had increased to $1.2 billion.[35] For their money, corporations receive access to professors' research and offices, even though the professors' salaries are principally paid by students and taxpayers.

University administrators have facilitated corporate access. MIT came up with a method of directly selling faculty expertise rather than having its professors walking the streets on their own. MIT established the Industrial Liaison Program (ILP), which charges 300 corporations from $10,000 to $50,000 per year in membership fees. For the fees, corporations get access to research reports written by MIT faculty, access to 70 symposia and faculty seminars, and direct, personal access to MIT's faculty. As the ILP catalog describes it, MIT places "at the disposal of industry the expertise and resources of all the schools, departments and laboratories of MIT."[36]

The program encourages MIT professors to participate by using an inducement similar to the coupons on the top of Betty Crocker cake mixes. Faculty get "points" for their involvements with member corporations. The points that professors accumulate can be redeemed for travel to professional conferences, computer equipment, office furniture, or other "prizes." MIT awards each faculty member one point for each unpublished article that is made available to an ILP member, two points for a phone conversation or a brief campus meeting with a corporate member, and twelve points for a visit to a company's headquarters or lab. Each point is worth about $35 in prize money.

An investigation of the ILP by Congress in 1989 found that professors involved in the program had more contact with foreign than domestic corporations and that the majority of the foreign firms were Japanese. (The ILP has only one office outside of Cambridge, Massachusetts. That office is in Tokyo.) For $50,000, Japanese corporations receive access to about half-a-billion dollars in research that is conducted at MIT annually, of which 86 percent is funded by the U.S. government.

MIT has another program that ties the university more closely to industry than does the ILP. This program, called the New Products Program, is a joint project of the mechanical engineering, electrical engineering, and management departments. Corporations pay the university a fee of $500,000 to develop a new product for their company, and MIT promises to come up with a product within two years. Three faculty members and four graduate students are assigned to work on the product, and the students wind up devoting more than half of their study time to it. In effect, students pay MIT in order to work as apprentices on corporate research projects.

Similar programs exist at other universities, such as the Rensselaer Polytechnic Institute in Troy, New York, and the University of Texas. Rensselaer operates the Center for Product Innovation, which conducts research for corporate clients. Its funders—including Timex, General Dynamics, and Norelco—support the center with dues and monies for specific projects. One of the center's most widely heralded projects was redesigning a coffee pot for Norelco.[37] As another example, the University of Texas has the Center for Technology Venturing, which "implements cooperative faculty, graduate-student, and firm studies that enhance mutual understanding of the technology commercialization process." In practice this means that the center conducts research for corporate clients such as 3M, Ford, and Dell Computer Corporation.[38]

While universities argue that these corporate-academic relationships provide educational experiences for students, some clearly lack educational value. Administrators at Yale University, for example, are hard pressed to explain the educational value of the Institute for Biospheric Studies, which was established in 1990 with a $20 million endowment from Edward P. Bass. Bass is chairman of Space Biospheres Ventures, which operates the Biosphere 2 dome in the Arizona desert. The dome is a 3.15 acre enclosure that purports to be a self-contained ecosystem where scientific research is conducted. However, Yvonne Clearwater, an environmental psychologist for NASA, says the dome is "turning out to be nothing more than a tourist attraction." She asserts that it has little scientific value and is essentially "a kooky Disneyland."[39] Other critics have been even less charitable, charging the company with scientific fraud and quackery.[40]

Despite the pseudoscientific basis of "biospheric studies," Yale president Benno Schmidt accepted money for the institute, saying the "gift powerfully enhances Yale's capacity to meet its responsibilities for academic leadership in an area of utmost importance to the future of humanity and of the earth which is our home." Schmidt added that "we will be the best in this area, I have no doubt."[41] (Two years later, Schmidt resigned as president of Yale to work for Christopher Whittle, whose controversial Channel One news show brings commercials into high school classrooms.) Other universities, including the University of Arizona and Columbia University, have also struck up close ties with Bass and the biospherians. Columbia and Arizona professors, like those from Yale, also conduct "research" at the Disneyesque dome.[42]

Although the biospheric escapades of Yale, Columbia, and the University of Arizona might appear to be aberrations in the world of academe, in many ways, they are typical. Like numerous other universities, the University of Arizona, Yale, and Columbia also house centers and programs that push corporate and right-wing agendas. The University of Arizona has the Karl Eller Center for the Study of the Private Market Economy, which exists to conduct research bolstering free enterprise and to promote "meaningful interaction between the academic and corporate communities."[43] Yale has the John M. Olin Program in Law and Economics. A study released in May 1993 by a Washington-based public interest group called Alliance for Justice charged that the Law and Economics program was trying to shift judicial thinking to the political right by inviting judges to expenses-paid conferences that presented pro-corporate interpretations of civil law.[44] Columbia has a similar program that offers courses to law students rather than judges.[45]

Many other universities have centers and programs that are similar to the Karl Eller Center and the Olin program. Most of these are funded by the same corporations and conservative foundations that fund the National Association of Scholars, the American Enterprise Institute, and other groups that have proclaimed political correctness, not corporate investments, to be the major threat to academic freedom.

Rather than shedding light on what has happened to universities, the PC debate has succeeded in hiding what has happened. The debate has focused attention on the teaching of humanities at a few elite institutions, rather than on what has happened to the medicine, science, law, business, social science, and professional programs that train the vast majority of U.S. college students. An examination of what has happened in these disciplines reveals that the ivory towers of America have been leased by corporations, wealthy patrons, and right-wing foundations. Being "politically correct" in academia today means having an endowed chair or a lucrative consulting contract. It has nothing to do with being a left-wing zealot.

 Chapter Two

The CEOs: The College Executive Officers

On April Fool's Day 1994, Oklahoma senator David Boren denied media reports that he would be abdicating his posts on the Senate Finance and Agricultural, Nutrition, and Forestry committees to accept a position as president of the University of Oklahoma. "That's just incorrect," Boren said about the rumor of his impending departure from the Senate.[1] Three weeks later, the senator appeared at a press conference with his family, where he disclosed that he had fibbed on April Fool's Day.[2]

After leaving the Senate, Boren became president of the University of Oklahoma, making him the first Oklahoman to be governor, senator, and university president. Given the driving force at universities today—raising money from, and doing work for, corporations—Boren's choice as University of Oklahoma president was fitting. In the Senate, Boren had shaken the corporate money tree and voted for legislation that helped his campaign contributors, while denying that he accepted special interest money. Senator Boren refused to accept contributions from political action committees (PACs), and blasted other politicians who did, but nevertheless accepted large, individual donations from corporate moguls.[3]

Senator Boren was particularly skilled in prying open the wallets of oil company executives. During his 1990 Senate campaign, Boren got money from the heads of Phillips Petroleum, AMOCO, Bankoff Oil, Occidental Oil, and a gaggle of other energy czars.[4] And the senator served them well. When Boren announced that he was leaving Capitol Hill for the ivory tower, the *Tulsa World* lamented, "Energy to Lose Ally: Domestic Industry Not Looking Forward to Boren's Departure from Congress." The article quoted

Nicholas Bush, chief of the American Gas Association, who said that Boren's departure from the Senate was "a loss to the business community and the natural gas industry."[5]

As University of Oklahoma president, Boren will probably do pretty much the same thing that he did in the Senate: raise corporate money and then deny that the money has strings attached. However, as university president, Boren won't have to answer to angry, disbelieving voters.

Many other large universities have also appointed well-connected politicians, foundation executives, or former corporate chiefs as presidents. These people, like Boren, have the background and clout needed to convince corporate and foundation chiefs to invest in their universities. For example, Eamon M. Kelly, president of Tulane University in New Orleans since 1981, spent most of his adult life working for the Ford Foundation and the federal government before being named university executive vice president. After two years as executive vice president, Kelly was made president. Roland W. Schmitt, president of Rensselaer Polytechnic Institute between 1988 and 1993, was previously an executive with General Electric Corp. for 35 years.[6] In 1993, Michigan State University in East Lansing hired M. Peter McPherson as president. McPherson was previously group executive vice president of Bank of America in San Francisco. He was a special assistant to President Ford, administrator for the Agency for International Development, and Deputy Secretary of the Treasury in the Reagan administration before joining the Bank of America.[7]

These university presidents are the chief executive officers of their institutions, and their jurisdiction includes virtually everything that occurs on college campuses. They, along with other high-level administrators, are appointed by, and answer to, a board of trustees (sometimes called a board of regents) that is composed of successful alumni, industry leaders, political officials, and, particularly at public universities, an occasional union boss. "Corporate executives are the largest single group represented on governing boards of colleges and universities," observes University of California professor Ben Bagdikian.[8] These trustees, who are often hostile to intellectualism, pick administrators who share their attitudes and corporate worldview; they do not pick left-wingers, multiculturalists, or radical feminists, despite the claims of conservative critics like D'Souza, Kimball, and Balch.

The Board of Regents of the University of Minnesota, which is selected by the state legislature, typifies the composition of many state universities. Members include former governor Wendell Anderson, Ceridian Corp. CEO Lawrence Perlman, Medtronic Corp. vice president Bill Hogan, and Building Trades Council president David Roe. The Board of Trustees of New York University, on the other hand, is typical of high-priced, private universities. The board is headed by financier and CBS network owner Laurence Tisch. It also includes former Health, Education, and Welfare secretary Joseph Califano; Salomon Brothers brokerage firm founder William R. Salomon; real-estate-magnate-turned-publisher Mortimer Zuckerman; and tycoon Leonard Stern, who donated $30 million to NYU's business school, which is named after him. Of 55 trustees, 19 have law degrees, 10 have master-of-business-administration degrees, and 20 have either a bachelor's degree or no degree. Educators among NYU's trustees are rare.

The Boston University CEO: A Case Study

Despite the fact that university presidents make decisions affecting academe, they are selected entirely on the basis of their administrative experience and money-raising skills, not their academic experience. If scholarly accomplishments were the criterion for selecting administrators, few university presidents would be in office, including Boston University's John Silber.

Silber became Boston University's (BU) president in 1971, after working nearly a decade at the University of Texas as a department chair and dean. Like most university presidents, he became BU's president based on his administrative experience, not his scholarly achievements. Silber's published résumé reports that in 1960 he wrote one book, *The Ethical Significance of Kant's Religion*, and edited another, *Religion Within the Limits of Reason Alone*. This résumé is exaggerated: "The Ethical Significance of Kant's Religion," rather than being a book, was actually an introductory essay in a translation of Kant's *Religion Within the Limits of Reason Alone* (which Silber didn't translate, either.)[9] Other tales about Silber's academic accomplishments are equally exaggerated.[10]

Although Silber's scholarly achievements are wimpish, he is an iron-pumping fund raiser, having increased the university's endowment nineteenfold, to $371 million from just $19 million.[11] Unfortunately for students, few of the dollars that Silber raises have trickled down to them. If anything, the dollars trickled upward. BU's tuition tripled during the past decade, going from $5,515 per year in 1980-81 to a staggering $15,950 per year, as BU's debt increased thirtyfold and its academic infrastructure weakened.[12] And much of the grant and corporate money that Silber brought to the university during this period undermined, rather than enhanced, the academic integrity of BU's programs, by moving professors out of the classroom and into the laboratory and field—sometimes as far away as Pakistan. At BU's College of Communication, for example, Silber insisted that the college work on a $500,000 grant from the United States Information Agency to teach journalism techniques to Afghan *mujahedin* based in Pakistan. The program was to be run during 1987 with the Hearst Corp.'s King Features, but Hearst withdrew from the project after American Society of Newspaper Editors president Michael Gartner accused it of "being in bed with the U.S. propaganda agency."[13] BU went ahead with the project, despite opposition to it within the communication college.

As a result of this insistence on going ahead with the program, the dean of the communication college resigned. He was replaced by H. Joaquim Maitre, a right-wing refugee from East Germany who had no academic credentials in the communication field but who strongly supported the Afghan training project. Bernice Buresh, a former reporter and journalism professor, resigned after she and other opponents of the program were harassed by Maitre and other administrators. Maitre even wore a mask to a forum on academic freedom where Buresh spoke.[14]

Such actions by Silber and his underlings have not helped the reputation of BU's College of Communication. Although the university insists that it has one of the top communication programs in the country, BU wasn't listed as a leading school of communication in several published rankings.[15] And other parts of BU's infrastructure are not in much better shape. For example, BU has one of the most meagerly funded libraries among research universities. Its library was ranked 66th among university libraries in the United States by the *Chronicle of Higher Education.* BU's library expenditures in 1991-92 were lower than those of Louisiana State University and about the same as those of the University of South Carolina. The number of volumes in its library is slightly lower than at Auburn University in Auburn, Alabama, an institution better known—and properly so—for its football team than for its academics.[16]

Despite this lack of attention to BU's academic infrastructure, Silber has seen to it that money from an assortment of right-wing foundations has made it into BU's bank accounts. The money is used for operating several on-campus, conservative "think tanks"—such as the Center for Defense Journalism, the Disinformation Documentation Center, and the Institute for the Study of Ideology, Conflict and Policy—which produce and distribute propaganda labelled as academic research. Some of the foundation money is also used to underwrite classes, such as "Reporting Military Affairs," that provide right-wing indoctrination rather than instruction. "Reporting Military Affairs," which is taught in the Journalism Department, is designed "to make journalists more sympathetic to the military," not to produce good reporters, a BU professor observed.[17]

Although such right-wing propaganda centers and courses abound on BU's campus, Silber has attempted to keep new intellectual trends—such as critical theory, feminism, and multiculturalism—from entering the campus. As Silber put it, "We have resisted the fad toward critical legal studies. In the English Department and departments of literature, we have not allowed the structuralists or the deconstructionists to take over. We have resisted revisionist history...We have not fallen into the clutches of the multiculturalists."[18] In effect, Silber has made sure that conservative, pro-corporate ideas dominate BU's academic environment.

This corporate influence is reflected in the university's endowed chairs. As of July 1, 1991, BU had 44 endowed professorships, funded by corporations, fat cats, and alumni. The largest number of these are in the medical school and have names like the Sterling Drug Visiting Professor of Medicine, the Sandson Chair in Health Manpower, and the Waterhouse Professor in Anatomy.[19]

Corporations have not been alone in adding to BU's coffers. BU has also received substantial pork-barrel handouts from the federal government, which were obtained through lobbying, political conniving, and back-scratching. Pork-barrel handouts are acquired by such methods as having a friendly politician attach a special appropriation to a bill making its way through Congress. The special appropriation earmarks money for a specific project at a university. Of all universities, BU was the second-highest recipient of pork-barrel appropriations in 1992, receiving $29 million in federally earmarked money that year.[20]

Boston University has rewarded the government's pork-barrel largess by charging one of the highest overhead rates among universities on federal grants that it receives. Overhead rates represent expenses that universities incur when conducting research that goes beyond the cost of the research itself. BU has a whopping 62 percent overhead rate for grants, whereas the majority of universities have overhead rates under 50 percent. The University of Iowa, the University of Wisconsin, and Pennsylvania State University have average overhead rates of 44 percent.[21]

Although John Silber has done little to improve BU's academic infrastructure, he has nevertheless been lavishly rewarded by BU's board of trustees, some of whom have benefited financially from Silber's money-hustling.[22] During the 1991-92 academic year, Silber received $414,715 in salary and bonuses.[23] Of this amount, $275,000 was salary and $139,715 was benefits. During 1992-93, Silber received a $300,000 bonus in addition to a salary of $337,500 and $139,463 in benefits, making his total compensation package a whopping $776,963.[24] Besides his salary and benefits, Silber also received other perquisites, including a $638,000 loan at little or no interest, a $138,000 interest-free loan to purchase a fashionable brownstone residence at a below-market price, a university-owned home in which he also resides, a car and driver, an entertainment budget, and a $2.3 million insurance policy.[25] The university also paid Silber $386,700 from profits that were made from selling Seradyn stocks, in which the university had invested. Silber says that he returned this money to the university.[26]

The Same Mold

As is true of other university presidents, Silber's salary and perks are based on his having brought money into the university's coffers, even though the money does not enhance BU's academic programs. Universities consistently mention such fund raising, not academic accomplishments, as the justification for administrators' six-figure salaries. For example, to explain his $167,000 compensation package, President George M. Harmon of Millsaps College in Jackson, Mississippi noted that under his leadership the college's endowment had increased more than tenfold, and that he had run two successful fund-raising campaigns that netted $47 million.[27] However, this fund raising hasn't translated into improved education or lower tuition for Millsaps students. By most standard measures of educational excellence, such as student-faculty ratio and incoming students' ACT scores, Millsaps was performing much the same in 1990-91 as in 1980-81, despite the larger endowment and huge tuition increases. Between 1980 and 1991, Millsaps's tuition went from $3,000 to $8,250.[28]

Other university presidents are also well-compensated for being successful fund raisers. During Columbia University president Michael Sovern's 13 years as CEO, for instance, the university's endowment nearly quadrupled to $1.9 billion.[29] At the time that Sovern resigned as president because of his wife's illness, he was receiving a salary of $363,600 and $46,199 in benefits. As in the case of Millsaps, despite the quadrupling of Columbia's endowment, tuition at the university also soared.[30]

The University of Pennsylvania and Tufts University in Medford, Massachusetts provide further examples. In 1993, Penn launched a fund-raising drive and selected a new president. The fund-raising effort was successful, pushing Penn's endowment up to $1.35 billion, and so was the presidential search. Judith Rodin, a Penn graduate, was named president. At the time that Rodin's appointment was announced, Alvin Shoemaker, who headed the presidential search committee and the board of trustees, announced that Rodin's "main job will be keeping the momentum [of the fund raising] going."[31] Similarly, Michigan State University president John DiBiaggio was selected as president of Tufts University primarily because of his "proven fund raising abilities," a Tufts spokesperson reported.[32]

The six-figure salaries given to these university presidents are the norm, even at colleges with just a few thousand students. A study conducted by the *Chronicle of Higher Education* of salaries received by university CEOs found that 15 major private research universities—including Columbia, New York, and Johns Hopkins universities—paid their CEOs more than $300,000, and just two of 33 research universities paid their CEOs less than $200,000.[33] According to the College and University Personnel Association, the average salary of presidents at research universities was $141,000 in 1991, a 22-percent increase since 1988. By contrast, faculty salaries rose less than 10 percent during the same period.[34] Not far behind these figures for research universities, the average salary of presidents at private, nonreligious universities was $113,627. This average includes the salaries paid to CEOs at small institutions such as Goucher College in Towson, Maryland and Hollins College in Hollins, Virginia. Such small colleges comprise the majority of higher-education institutions.

The university presidents who make salaries in the low six figures can and do supplement their incomes by sitting on the boards of directors of corporations, for which they are handsomely paid. University trustees view these board appointments positively because they draw universities and corporations closer together. Approximately 10 percent of university presidents sit on such boards.[35] City University of New York chancellor W. Ann Reynolds, for example, receives around $158,000 from the university in salary—more than the governor of New York makes—but also sits on the boards of Abbott Laboratories, Owen-Corning Fiberglass, American Electric Power, Humana, Inc., and Maytag Corp. She received $140,000 in 1993 from these corporations.[36]

What accounts for such lavish compensation and access to outside income? One explanation given for the large salaries paid to university administrators is that universities now compete with corporations for executives, because both are in essentially the same business. University presidents, like corporate CEOs, are in the revenue-production and R&D business, not in the business of educating students. As some education observers told the *Chronicle of Higher Education*, universities "must pay their top officials salaries that are competitive with the corporate world if they are to attract the best people."[37] President Stephen Trachtenberg of George Washington University in Washington, D.C.—a former federal official, BU administrator under John Silber, and board member of the

Loctite Corp., MNC Financial, and Security Trust Co.—claims that "university presidents work harder than their opposite numbers in the corporate world and are compensated less."[38]

What Trachtenberg, who received over $300,000 in salary and benefits in 1991, didn't mention is that university presidents get perquisites available to few corporate CEOs. The salaries and the perks that university presidents get—and flaunt—has contributed to a culture of greed on college campuses that makes the sacking of savings and loans look like philanthropy. In more ways than one, university presidents, in fact, resemble the CEOs of corrupt savings and loans. For example, university CEOs cover up fraud within their institutions, harass and dismiss whistleblowers, lavishly spend university funds on themselves, and invest their institutions' money in ways that are detrimental to their primary constituents. In the case of universities, these primary constituents are the taxpayers and students who get little from universities' R&D expenditures.

The entire atmosphere of a university is affected by the conduct of its president. University professors learn from the behavior of their CEOs that the academic tower is not scaled by good teaching or dedicated scholarship, but by pandering to corporate needs and glad-handing tycoons.

The Culture of Greed

The culture of greed appears in numerous ways in a university CEO's life. For instance, most university presidents receive free housing (usually in a university-owned mansion), maid services, entertainment and travel budgets, and numerous small benefits (such as free tickets to theater performances and sporting events, and box seats at bowl games.) As a fairly minor example of such benefits, the University of Wisconsin president, chancellor, vice chancellor, and board of regents went to Pasadena, California to see their football team play in the 1994 Rose Bowl. This junket cost $122,475, which was paid out of the university's share of Rose Bowl revenues.[39]

Another manifestation of this culture is paid access to private clubs. In Illinois, for example, presidents of state-run universities have received private club memberships and thousands of dollars in expense accounts. At Northern Illinois University in De Kalb, President Clyde Wingfield's membership to the Coral Reef Yacht Club in Miami, Florida was paid by the university foundation. The president of the University of Illinois has memberships at the Champaign Country Club, the Tavern Club, and the University Club in Chicago that are paid for by the university foundation. (He also has a university-furnished maid, car, and home.)[40] The Illinois universities claim that such perquisites are legitimate business expenses, because these clubs are locations where presidents wine and dine potential donors, who are accustomed to such luxury.

Other instances of greed involve sweetheart deals and princely expenses. For example, President George W. Johnson of George Mason University in Fairfax, Virginia was sold "a choice piece of residential real estate" by a financial patron of the university for $50,000 less than its market value. Johnson intends to build a retirement home on the property. John T. Hazel, Jr., the developer and university patron who sold Johnson the property, said that he "wanted to make a gift to George Johnson," whom he considers his friend.[41] After buying the property, Johnson worked on a political campaign with Hazel to unseat the chair of the Fairfax County Board of Supervisors, who sought to limit growth and development in the county.[42]

At Central Missouri State University in Warrensburg, the president used university funds to take his wife and son to Europe and the Bahamas. In the Bahamas, the president and his family ran up a $4,709 hotel and meal tab. Stating that "these are not vacation junkets," university spokespeople defended the trip as university business, since the president went to the Bahamas to see the university basketball team play and scouted out the possibility of establishing education programs in Europe.[43]

Other presidents have incurred far more lavish expenses. Northern Illinois University president Clyde Wingfield, for example, spent $100,000 remodeling his 5,000-square-foot presidential mansion, and another $16,000 on his presidential inauguration. Wingfield skirted state laws requiring approval of large expenditures by "breaking the remodeling project down into small parts to get around having to receive approval for the work."[44] Similarly, former University of Minnesota president Kenneth Keller spent nearly $1.7 million renovating the presidential mansion and his university office. The renovations were paid for out of a "slush fund" that Keller controlled, whose existence was unknown to the board of regents. Like Wingfield, he violated a policy requiring costly expenditures to be approved by the regents.[45] Wingfield and Keller were both forced to resign, but not because of their extravagance; rather, they were punished for failing to comply with procedures that governed spending.

Even when, as with Wingfield and Keller, a university official's extravagance leads (at least indirectly) to termination, he or she may still manage to continue plundering university funds. In some cases, administrators have finagled large severance packages when under pressure to resign. At the University of Colorado, for example, Chancellor Glendon Drake was asked to resign by the university president because he was "inaccessible" and had made questionable expenditures. In return for resigning, Drake received a severance package of $232,400. University trustees and the president even misled state legislators into believing that the severance package was only $101,000; and the real amount was not discovered until the *Rocky Mountain News* went to court and forced the university to reveal it.[46]

Many other examples of questionable severance packages exist. In one incident at the University of California, exiting President David P. Gardner received a "golden parachute" worth almost $1 million. The retirement package was put together by another administrator, Ronald Brady, whom Gardner secretly gave an extra full-year's pay the day before leaving office. The extra pay amounted to $181,640.[47]

The golden parachutes, luxurious living, and large salaries of university presidents put them in the same class with corporate mandarins. And mimicking corporate CEOs' relations with their employees, university presidents rarely have any contact with the professors and staff members of their institutions. Similarly, they almost never meet with students. Instead, their contacts are limited to other CEOs, other university administrators, and members of the bureaucracy who assist them with fund raising—all to the detriment of the quality of education.

The Bulging Bureaucracies for Fund Raising

During the 1980s, colleges and universities hired more non-teaching staff than professors. The number of full-time professors at universities increased by 8.6 percent between 1985 and 1990, while the non-teaching staff grew by 13 percent. By 1990, professors accounted for under 30 percent of full-time university employees. At many universities—including Swarthmore College in Swarthmore, Pennsylvania, a faculty-intensive institution with one faculty member for every eight students—only one-fourth of each student's tuition dollars goes toward faculty salaries.[48]

The fastest-growing category of non-teaching staff was "professionals," which includes accountants, athletic coaches, bookkeepers, and fund raisers, most of whom are involved in the university money chase. The number of university-employed professionals grew a whopping 28.1 percent during the late 1980s. At some institutions, the growth was even faster. At Alma College in Alma, Michigan, the number of faculty and students remained nearly constant between 1975 and 1990, but the number of grant administrators, who supervise the procurement and spending of grant monies, tripled.[49]

These professionals make only marginal contributions—if that—to the primary function of universities, which is educating students. Instead, they function as the go-betweens for the university and corporations that contract with the university for services.

Typical of these newly created professional jobs is "director of the university-industry research program" at the University of Wisconsin at Madison. An advertisement for the position stated that the director's responsibilities include "encouraging University researchers to transfer technologies with commercial potential to the private sector, encouraging private sector support of University research, overseeing the awarding and administration of the Applied Research funds, [and] communicating University research capabilities to the private sector." In effect, the advertisement was for a high-paid hustler, who could sell university research and research findings to corporations. Most of the newly added professional jobs at universities are similar.

These professionals answer directly to university administrators and are largely unconcerned with the quality of teaching or scholarship. Instead, they serve as an inertial force, propelling universities closer and closer to corporations, wealthy patrons, and foundations. Their job is to cultivate ties with industry and fat cats, and their salaries and continued employment depend on their successful promotion of university-industry ties. If universities were to decide to return to their primary function of teaching, rather than be involved in research endeavors that benefit corporate America, the legions of professional fund raisers on college campuses would certainly do everything possible to assure that university-corporate ties continued.

This proclivity of bureaucrats for fund raising is demonstrated by Dorin Schumacher, founder and director of the Office of Industry Relations at Purdue University in Lafayette, Indiana. Schumacher wrote a book titled *Get Funded!* that "shows how the university-industry linkage can be accomplished." The book claims that the problem with universities isn't "the destruction of values either by corporate support for academic research or by university-industry partnerships"; the problem is the "disincentives built into university bureaucracies that discourage faculty and prevent even greater interaction with business." The way to reduce these disincentives is to create an industrial relations office on campus. "Having access to an industry relations service can have a positive effect on faculty attitudes toward working with the corporate sector," Schumacher writes. According to Schumacher, evidence from Scotland and Mexico (of all places!) indicates that an on-campus service that provides "industrial liaison assistance both decreases faculty resistance and hostility to the idea of entering into contact with industry and stimulates faculty interest in establishing industrial research linkages."[50]

The Game

Even when their job descriptions do not specifically mention fund raising—as is the case with athletic coaches—these professionals know that their primary responsibility is revenue raising. To be successful revenue raisers, coaches need to field winning teams that fill stadiums, inspire alumni donations, and get into lucrative, televised post-season games. The bowl games, in particular, have become very lucrative because of corporate sponsorship. Corporate names and logos adorn most post-season football games. There are the Builder's Square Alamo Bowl, IBM OS/2 Fiesta Bowl, USF&G Sugar Bowl, Federal Express Orange Bowl, Mobil Cotton Bowl, and CompUSA Florida Citrus Bowl. By 1988, football teams playing in bowl games received a minimum of $500,000 each. Teams playing in the NCAA "final four" basketball playoffs earn over $1 million, and teams playing in the Rose Bowl receive about $6 million.[51]

Thus, coaches try to field winning teams at almost any cost— including such unethical practices as paying student athletes, making false promises to recruit high school stars, and pressuring faculty to pass failing athletes. All of these and other questionable practices have been widely reported by the media. An "executive director of the NCAA estimated that 30 percent of major college programs are involved in illegal activities,"[52] such as allowing wealthy alumni to shower gifts on student athletes.

Like college presidents, successful coaches receive huge salaries that dwarf those paid to even the highest-paid professors. In *College Sports, Inc.*, Murray Sperber estimated that at least 50 college football and basketball coaches are paid more than a quarter-million dollars annually. The average income for "the 150 NCAA Division I men's basketball coaches and 100 Division I-A football coaches tops $100,000," Sperber reports.[53] When television contracts, summer pay, contracts with sporting goods manufacturers and other corporations, and other income are included, the pay of top coaches often tops $500,000 a year. Coaches get these salaries because they generate big money for universities.

Where Has All the Money Gone?

The irony of higher "education" is that little of the money that college presidents, technology-transfer managers, coaches, think tanks, grants officers, and development experts (a fancy name for fund raisers) take in actually goes to education. Rather than going to educational programs, money is used to pay for labs, equipment, and facilities needed to procure more grants or to expand that portion of the bureaucracy that has brought in the money. For example, money generated by sports teams tends to be spent by university athletic departments for coaches' salaries, recruitment, travel, equipment, promotions, and a host of other department expenses. The only education-related contributions that sports teams make to universities are in the form of their athletes' tuition, which athletic departments frequently, though not always, pay. The small amount of money left over after payment of these expenses is then used to cover the losses sustained by sports, such as baseball, that generate little income from ticket sales or broadcasting rights. Any remaining money—usually there is none—remains in athletic department coffers.

University think tanks, such as the Hoover Institution at Stanford University, operate in exactly the same manner as athletic departments. They raise huge amounts of money that they spend on themselves, rather than on education. For example, the Hoover Institution received $7.5 million in gifts, $3.7 million in endowment contributions, and over $4 million in Stanford University funding during 1990-91; but it never spent a nickel on education. Its $19 million budget was spent entirely on research and publications, on its library and archives, and on administration.[54] Despite the Hoover Institution's neglect of education, one of its representatives had the effrontery to criticize professors in a *Washington Post* op-ed article for "shamefully neglecting teaching and producing reams of trivial, irrelevant research."[55]

Technology transfer, or the licensing of discoveries made by university researchers to corporations, also produces little revenue for education. Not only do universities pay the staff of their technology-transfer offices—which include secretaries, managers, and lawyers—but they usually split their royalties with the professors responsible for the discoveries. (Technology-transfer offices are discussed more fully in Chapter Three.) Universities must also pay the cost of filing patent applications, most of which fail to produce any licenses. The result is that "many universities lose money on technology transfer programs, at least initially," reports the *Seattle Times*.[56] Universities that do make money from technology transfer usually plow the money right back into research centers or corporate parks, rather than into education.

The few universities that do take in substantial revenues as a result of licensing usually make their profits from one major discovery, rather than many small ones. And the amount that these universities make is often less than expected. The number of truly lucrative licensing agreements can be counted on the fingers of one person's hands. They include the license shared by Stanford and the University of Wisconsin for recombinant DNA technology, Michigan State's patent on cisplatin, the University of Washington's breakthrough treatment for hepatitis B, and the University of Florida's royalties from Gatorade. In the latter case, the university makes only about $2 million in royalties, despite Gatorade's sales of $500 to $600 million annually. The director of the University of Florida's office of corporate programs has lamented that "if we had done Gatorade right, we would be getting $5 or $6 million...It is a classic example of how not to handle a patent idea."[57]

Despite the costs of technology transfer and the low probability of making money on it, university administrators continue to bet on patents to raise revenues, just as the lumpen proletariat continues to waste its few dollars on lottery tickets and horse races. (This focus on research and development also allows university administrators to demand comparable pay to corporate CEOs.) Moreover, the money lost on technology-transfer programs does not even include the money initially spent by universities on the research that ultimately led to the patents, and this is the most costly part of the process. Increasingly, high-tech discoveries require very expensive laboratory facilities, and universities have poured huge amounts of money into building such facilities. The amount of money that grants generate rarely covers these massive expenses, so universities embark on fund-raising campaigns or divert tuition dollars to cover these costs.

Tuition also subsidizes research in a much less visible (though equally expensive) way, according to a 1992 congressional subcommittee report.[58] Professors who conduct research—even research not even partially subsidized by grants—are usually given reduced teaching assignments. Some universities, such as the University of Minnesota, have reduced teaching requirements across the board to encourage professors to do "research."

Because many professors spend their time conducting research rather than teaching, the number of students in each class has increased, and additional professors have been hired to teach the classes formerly taught by the researchers. The newly hired professors are also expected do to research, and their teaching requirements must therefore also be reduced. This self-perpetuating cycle explains why the number of professors has grown much faster than the number of students. Between 1980 and 1989, student enrollment increased just 10.9 percent, whereas the number of college instructors increased by 20.1 percent.[59] During the same period, class sizes also increased, rather than decreasing as might have been expected. At some universities, including Michigan State, the University of Wisconsin, and the University of Minnesota, many classes have several hundred students in them. At the University of Illinois at Urbana, a political science course had 1,156 students.[60]

The increased number of professors explains why gross professorial salary costs at universities have increased substantially at the same time that the salaries of individual professors, particularly in the social sciences and humanities, have increased only modestly.[61] It also explains why tuition rates have increased faster than the costs of medical care, housing, or inflation.

 Chapter Three

Sharing Biomedical Knowledge: From University Researcher to Corporate Shareholder

During the early decades of the Cold War, the U.S. military and intelligence services commissioned university biomedical researchers to conduct much covert, ethically questionable research. These projects severely compromised medical research ethics and, in so doing, helped prepare university researchers for the ethical compromises that they would later make when doing work for corporations.

During the 1940s and 1950s, for example, the Atomic Energy Commission paid medical researchers at MIT and Vanderbilt University in Nashville, Tennessee to expose more than 110 mentally retarded children and hundreds of pregnant women to radioactive materials.[1] In another case, between 1960 and 1971 the Defense Department funded University of Cincinnati researchers to expose 88 patients to radioactivity. University experimenters contend that the experiments tested whether radiation could slow tumor growth, but critics of the program charge that the tests were to determine the effects of radiation exposure on troops. More than 50 of these patients were Black; many were poor. The subjects were told that there was a "risk" associated with participation in the study, but were never informed that there was a one-in-four chance of dying.[2]

In still other instances, psychiatric patients at the University of Missouri and University of Minnesota were given LSD in experiments conducted for the U.S. Air Force. And Tulane University researchers implanted electrodes in the brains of mental patients before giving them LSD and other drugs in a study conducted for the U.S. Army.[3]

Privatizing Medical Research

Since the 1980s, such military spending on biochemical research has declined, and university medical researchers have increasingly looked to large corporations to make up for the drop in government funding. This decline has actually brought researchers some unexpected benefits. Not only is corporate research far more lucrative than government-funded research, but it is also far less likely to be closely scrutinized by journalists or other investigators, who embarrassed many university medical schools by exposing their Cold War experiments. And regardless of who funds university biomedical research, universities can try to sell important research findings to pharmaceutical or biotech corporations as part of "technology transfer." Most large universities now have offices and administrators who specialize in technology transfer.

At the University of Wisconsin at Milwaukee (UWM), for example, the Office of Industrial Research and Technology Transfer works "with UWM faculty and area business and industry...in order to convert research results obtained in the university into commercial products, processes, and services."[4] The university not only licenses research findings to corporations, but also does contract work directly for corporations on new product development, customized testing and analysis, or anything else that brings in money. UWM's clients include Pharmacia Biochemicals, Inc., G. D. Searle, Siemens Medical Systems, and Miller Brewing Co.

Presidents of universities are proud of these technology transfer programs. University of Minnesota president Nils Hasselmo, for instance, wanted the public to know that his university was ranked sixth in licensing technologies to corporations, and was frustrated that the public didn't know this. The university had licensed 200 technologies to 150 corporations between 1986 and 1991.[5]

The chase for corporate dollars has even compelled some universities to move beyond simply transferring research patents through offices of technology transfer. Harvard University's Institutes of Medicine, for example, is establishing a research center where university biomedical researchers will work side by side with corporate researchers. Four floors of the institute's ten-story building will be reserved for corporate offices and researchers. The corporate employees will try to find lucrative ways to market the discoveries made by Harvard researchers, who will work on the other six floors. Some of the research that Harvard professors conduct will be financed by the Harvard-based corporations; other funding will come from the U.S. government, which currently gives Harvard Medical School and its affiliates $350 million of its $600 million annual budget.[6]

This deal produces many winners. Harvard will own the patents for the discoveries that its researchers make, and the Harvard-based corporations will be allowed to market the products. Harvard administrators hope that the licensing fees paid to Harvard will produce continuous income for the university. Harvard professors will also benefit because they will be allowed to become equity holders in the corporations, as well as to work for the corporations as paid consultants. The big losers in this deal, however, are communities that will subsidize most of the research with their taxes but will not benefit financially from their investment. Although Harvard is operating what amounts to a commercial venture, its nonprofit status shields it from paying corporate taxes at the expense of its local communities.

Several other university medical schools—including those at Baylor University in Waco, Texas, Johns Hopkins University in Baltimore, the University of California at Irvine, Maryland, and Columbia—also have ambitious plans for forging ties to corporations. However, none of these plans is as ambitious as that of the Scripps Research Institute, a nonprofit academic research center. Indeed, Scripps's plan may well represent the future of corporate-university ties. In 1992, the Scripps Institute agreed to give the Switzerland-based Sandoz Pharmaceutical Corporation, a large multinational company, the rights to all of Scripps's discoveries for the next ten years. In return for a grant of $300 million, Scripps agreed to give Sandoz a majority of seats on Scripps's Joint Scientific Council, access to research findings even before the National Institutes of Health gets them, and licenses for marketing Scripps's discoveries.[7]

The agreement resulted in two congressional subcommittees examining the deal, and eventually to renegotiations between Scripps and Sandoz.[8] According to U.S. Rep. Ron Wyden (D-OR), the

Scripps-Sandoz agreement meant that U.S. tax dollars would be financing research available exclusively to one foreign corporation. Wyden said that he hoped to prevent deals such as this from "becoming the wave of the future," whereby "universities will be falling over each other to wear the letter sweater of a big company."[9]

If Wyden wanted to stave off agreements similar to the one between Scripps and Sandoz, his actions were too little and too late. In December 1992, the Dana-Farber Institute, a Harvard University teaching hospital, announced that it was giving Sandoz the commercial rights to its potentially very profitable discovery of a method for identifying a mutant gene that causes colon cancer, one of the three most frequently occurring cancers. The mutant gene research was primarily funded by the U.S. government, but the rights are going to Sandoz because of a $100 million deal that the Harvard institute had cut with Sandoz. Sandoz gave Dana-Farber a ten-year, $100 million grant for research on cancer drugs. The agreement specified that anyone who accepted Sandoz money must give Sandoz licensing rights to the research findings. Although Sandoz money was not used for the colon cancer gene research, one of the researchers who discovered the mutant gene had received Sandoz money for a different project. That funding gave Sandoz the rights to the colon gene research.[10]

The Dana-Farber-Sandoz research agreement is but one of many similar agreements that have been signed by universities and corporations during the past decade and a half. Monsanto Corp. provided Washington University with a $23.5 million grant for research on proteins and peptides; Harvard University and Dupont signed a $6 million agreement for genetic research; the University of California at San Diego signed a $20 million agreement with Ciba-Geigy for research on arthritis; and Mallinkrodt, Inc. and Washington University signed a $3.8 million deal for research on artificial cells.[11]

While most of these corporate-university agreements are designed to provide income to companies and universities—frequently at the public's expense—not all work out amiably. Eli Lilly and Company filed suit against the University of California in 1993, charging that the university breached a contract giving it the rights to a bovine growth hormone that enhanced milk production. According to Lilly, it paid the university $1.6 million for research on the growth hormone, and the licensing rights to the hormone therefore belonged to the company. Instead of turning the hormone over to Lilly, however, the university's technology transfer office, in an effort to secure the highest price, invited Lilly and three other companies to bid on the licensing rights. Lilly then filed suit in an attempt to stop competitive bidding for the licensing.[12]

Big Business, Bigger Compromises

In addition to receiving corporate monies to finance their research, biomedical researchers frequently receive stocks or stock options from the corporations for which they do research. These corporate shares function as an incentive. The stocks and options allow the researcher to invest in the company at below-market value. If the researcher makes an "important discovery," the stocks soar in value, and the researcher becomes rich or, at the least, better-off financially.[13]

At the University of Minnesota, for example, Professor Fitz Bach received nearly $500,000 in stock and perks from Endotronics when he was conducting grant-funded research for the company. Bach's research abruptly ended when Endotronics was accused of bilking investors and falsifying sales reports. Another University of Minnesota scientist, Dr. David Knowlton, was the leading stockholder in Curative Technologies, Inc., which marketed Procuren, a wound-healing drug. Knowlton used university facilities to conduct research on Procuren for nearly a decade.[14]

These incentives can corrupt the integrity of scientific research in several ways. At Harvard University, for instance, Dr. Scheffer Teng tested a vitamin A ointment produced by Spectra Pharmaceutical Services and found the ointment ineffective. But Teng and his supervisor, Kenneth Kenyon, were both large stockholders in Spectra Pharmaceutical; and when Spectra went public in 1985, they tried to cover up the ointment's ineffectiveness by altering the placebo, changing doses, treating patients with additional drugs, and adding unauthorized subjects to the experiment. According to the *Boston Globe*, Teng succeeded in hiding the test results until he and his relatives had made more than $1 million from selling their Spectra stock.[15]

Another kind of corruption is the potential for scientists conducting research for companies to use their medical knowledge as "insider information." In this case, if a drug looks in clinical trials as though it will be effective, the researchers involved in these trials can quickly buy stocks in the company, hoping that the stocks will go up in value.

Stock ownership also encourages researchers to skew reports. Because researchers own stocks in companies they work for, they benefit financially from published research reports that praise the company's products. If an article reports that a trial drug looks promising, the stock values of the drug company shoot up. This occurred in the case of Genetech, a biotech corporation. In 1985, an article in the *New England Journal of Medicine* reported that a new drug, Genetech's t-PA, was twice as effective as a competing drug in dissolving blood clots. The article contained no mention that t-PA could cause bleeding or had no greater effect than the competing drug on the functioning of the left ventricle, a more important predictor of mortality than blood clotting. At least five members of the team of researchers who wrote the article owned stock in Genetech. The article resulted in Genetech's stock going from $18 per share in December 1984 to $28 per share in April 1985, the month that the article appeared. Subsequent studies reported the negative effects of t-PA, which the original researchers eventually acknowledged and reported.

Because of the conflicting reports, the National Institutes of Health provided grant funding for more studies to clarify t-PA's effectiveness. Several of the researchers who applied for and received the NIH funding also turned out to be Genetech stockholders, a fact that wasn't known when they received the grants. Their research showed the Genetech product to be more beneficial than did the other studies.[16]

Conflicts of Interest and Consulting

In addition to receiving research money and owning corporate stocks, many university medical researchers receive corporate monies for their expert testimony at government hearings, for consulting, and for speeches given on behalf of corporations. According to Professor Sheldon Krimsky of Tufts University, who studies the commercial penetration of university science departments, over 30 percent of MIT's biomedical faculty have business ties with biotech companies. Nearly 20 percent of Stanford and Harvard biomedical professors also have corporate ties through stock ownership, consulting, or speaking fees.[17] Krimsky estimates that over half of the biomedical researchers who belong to the prestigious National Academy of Sciences have corporate ties.[18]

Although biomedical researchers at universities try to portray consulting as a benign method for "underpaid" medical professors to make extra money, medical researchers are not underpaid, nor is their work necessarily benign. On the contrary, medical professors are often the highest-paid employees of universities, earning more than top administrators (including presidents and chancellors). At Tulane University, for example, President Eamon Kelly made $311,265 in salary and benefits during 1991. By contrast, an assistant professor of orthopedics was paid $639,254, a professor of orthopedics was paid $584,648, and the chair of the ophthalmology department was paid $563,620. At Columbia University, the highest-paid professors are also at the medical school. Columbia's president made $409,799 in salary and benefits in 1990, but an assistant professor of surgery was paid $1,157,154. The other top-paid employees at Columbia were also with the medical school.[19]

Not all medical professors are as well paid, but they do have some of the highest average incomes in the United States, even before their consulting dollars and dividends are counted. The average salary of professors of anesthesiology, a middle-income specialization in the medical field, was $196,100 in 1991. The average salary of professors of thoracic and cardio-vascular surgery was $422,800. Professors of plastic surgery averaged $284,700.[20] The lowest-paid assistant professors of medicine, on the other hand, are in community health, preventive medicine, and pediatrics, where assistant professors received an average salary of $82,900. Full professors received $119,500 on average. The lower pay of professors in these fields indicates where medical schools' priorities lie—certainly not with children or the poor.

Although highly paid by most standards, biomedical professors often supplement their incomes with corporate consulting. When these same medical researchers are expected to independently evaluate drugs for corporations from which they receive consulting monies, this consulting produces conflicts of interest. As a congressional investigation of scientific misconduct noted, consulting dollars give researchers an incentive to err in the direction of their corporate patrons, making it more likely that dangerous products will be released into the market.

Such a hazardous situation nearly occurred with research conducted for Centocor Corp., which sought to market a substance that could block the release of potentially lethal toxins produced by bacteria.[21]

In 1985, the late Drs. Henry Kaplan of Stanford University and Abraham Braude of the University of California at San Diego announced that they had discovered antibodies called HA-1A that bound to bacteria, thereby preventing the lethal effect of the bacteria's toxin in laboratory animals. Kaplan and Braude worked with two other researchers, Drs. Nelson Teng and Elizabeth Ziegler. In a typical case of "technology transfer," the antibody was licensed by Stanford and the University of California to Centocor, which named it "Centoxin."[22]

The next step was to develop Centoxin for commercial distribution. According to Centocor, the drug, if approved by the Food and Drug Administration (FDA), would be given to just under a half-million patients annually at $4,000 per treatment, making it an extremely profitable drug to produce. To test its effectiveness on humans, Centocor financed a study overseen by Professor Ziegler, who with Professor Teng also worked as a Centocor consultant.

In the February 14, 1991 issue of the prestigious *New England Journal of Medicine*, Ziegler and her associates announced that a multi-center clinical trial demonstrated that Centoxin "reduces mortality significantly in patients with sepsis and gram-negative bacteremia. The reduction in mortality was apparent as early as day 1 after treatment..."[23] According to the report, 49 percent of patients receiving a placebo died, compared to 30 percent receiving Centoxin. In more severely ill patients, the drug was even more effective. Fifty-seven percent receiving a placebo died, compared to just 33 percent receiving Centoxin.

As a result of this announcement, Centocor's stocks shot up in value. During the mid-1980s, the stock was worth just $12-$15 per share.[24] By January 1992, when it appeared that the drug was headed for FDA approval, Centocor stocks were valued at nearly $60 per share.

However, problems soon began to appear in the study to cool the market's enthusiasm. One problem with the Centocor-financed study was that the method of measuring effectiveness was changed during the course of the study. In addition, several other scientists were unable to reproduce the original laboratory results, which supposedly showed the efficacy of the antibody in animals. A study conducted by researchers with the National Institutes of Health found that dogs receiving Centoxin had even higher death rates than those that did not receive the antibody.

As a result of these and other results, the FDA decided against approving the drug. Instead, it reported that Centocor had violated scientific procedures with its analysis. The FDA ordered a second study, which Centocor began in 1992. The second study was abruptly ended in January 1993, when it showed that death rates among patients taking Centoxin were higher than among those taking a placebo—the opposite of what the first study had reported. Centocor stock plunged to under $6.50.[25]

The Centocor story is not an isolated incident. One of the best-known cases that shows how corporate consulting can produce conflicts of interest concerns Dr. Charles Bluestone, a professor of medicine at the University of Pittsburgh who was researching the effects of antibiotics on children's ear infections. During the period of his research, Bluestone received money from Eli Lilly and the Beecham Group, two pharmaceutical companies with a vested interest in his research. In 1985, he received $56,738 in honoraria and $29,008 for travel from them. He also received research funds from the companies.[26]

A congressional investigation into scientific conflicts of interest and misconduct found that Bluestone changed his method of diagnosing infections "in a way that made the drug under study look more efficacious." In published research reports, he failed to mention that the drug he tested was ineffective in some cases and that more than half of the infections that the drug supposedly "cured" recurred within six weeks. Contrary to government regulations, Dr. Bluestone also prevented his colleague, Dr. Erden Cantekin, from getting access to his research data, and then tried to stop publication of an article based on the data that concluded the drugs were ineffective.[27] Dr. Cantekin filed misconduct charges against Bluestone as a result of his actions; but the university dismissed them, claiming that the errors were simply oversights.

In fact, rather than taking action against Bluestone, the University of Pittsburgh struck out at Dr. Cantekin. A university committee investigated Cantekin's actions and charged him, not Bluestone, with scientific misconduct. The university concluded that the whistleblower was "uncollegial" and guilty of "serious violations of scientific and academic integrity." Moreover, the committee falsely charged that Cantekin had attempted to publish Bluestone's data as the official study of the antibiotic's effectiveness, rather than as a dissenting interpretation. The committee made these charges even though Cantekin had invited other researchers to co-author the paper with him and "notified the scientific journal where he had submitted his manuscript that his article was based on the same data described in the previously reviewed article by Bluestone and his colleagues."[28]

As a result of his whistleblowing, Cantekin was ousted from his university hospital office and given a windowless room above a Giant Eagle supermarket. The university also placed Cantekin on probation for five years. However, the U.S. congressional subcommittee examining scientific misconduct concluded that the University of Pittsburgh had retaliated against Cantekin because of his whistleblowing, not because of any scientific misconduct. The subcommittee reported that all of the charges directed against Cantekin were false.

The Veil of Silence

The reprisals against Dr. Cantekin indicate the lengths to which universities will go to protect corporate ties. Indeed, universities have consistently punished those who blow the whistle on university-corporate collusion and the compromise of scientific integrity. Many universities, fearing that exposure will result in the loss of grants, contracts, and other corporate funding, move quickly and vindictively to silence whistleblowers. If universities can quietly cover up misconduct, they are able to keep the grant money that would be lost if the misconduct became public.

The University of Minnesota has been one of the most consistent punishers of whistleblowers. James Zissler, a professor of microbiology, was removed from the university's ethics committee after he criticized medical faculty ties to industry. The university also denied his disability claim and tried to rescind his promotion to full professor, according to a $50,000 suit that Zissler filed against university administrators. Court papers filed by Zissler included a 46-page list of alleged wrongdoing at the university. University administrators denied Zissler's allegations and, of course, used taxpayer dollars to fight the suit.[29]

One of the administrators whom Professor Zissler named in his suit was Dr. John Najarian, the head of surgery at the medical school. Najarian's office was raided by investigators from the IRS and FBI on the morning of October 5, 1993, as part of an investigation into the production of antilymphocyte globulin (ALG), an antirejection drug used in kidney transplants. The federal government stopped the University of Minnesota from producing the drug, from which it made $10 million annually, because the university had failed to report serious side effects and deaths arising from the drug's use and had illegally made a profit from the sales.[30]

The raid was part of a larger probe seeking to determine whether Najarian's private medical practice group, which had offices at the university, had failed to pay taxes on its ALG profits. One director of the program, Richard Condie, had been fired earlier when an audit showed that he had collected $62,000 in consulting fees from a firm seeking to sell an ALG by-product.[31]

In another egregious case at Minnesota, two whistleblowers at the university were punished for complaining about Dr. Barry Garfinkel, the chief of child and adolescent psychiatry. One of the whistleblowers was a psychiatric nurse who reported that Garfinkel was using a blood test on autistic children that was not approved by the university's committee on human subjects. The nurse's charge turned out to be correct. But instead of disciplining Garfinkel, the university did nothing; and Garfinkel reprimanded the nurse, removed her from the study, and ultimately forced her resignation. The university stood by Garfinkel's actions.[32]

In the second instance involving Garfinkel, Michelle Rennie, a research assistant, accused Garfinkel of falsely claiming to have visited patients during a study of the effects of Anafranil, an antidepressant drug, on obsessive-compulsive children. The study was being conducted for Ciba-Geigy Corp., a Switzerland-based pharmaceutical firm that was seeking approval for the drug from the FDA. Ciba-Geigy was paying the university based on the number of patients studied and the number of clinical observations made, which added up to $250,000.

Rather than visiting patients himself, as he was required to do, Garfinkel ordered Rennie to do some examinations and skipped others. He also gave patients other drugs that could make Anafranil look more effective than it was, leading Rennie to complain about his actions. Rather than immediately disciplining Garfinkel, however, the university conducted a secret committee hearing that was chaired by one of Garfinkel's colleagues. Another member of the committee was also from Garfinkel's department. The committee concluded that there were "irregularities" in Garfinkel's research, but no misconduct on his part. The misconduct, the committee concluded, was by Rennie, whom it sought to discredit.

Rennie was charged with dishonesty and incompetence, even though her work evaluations were flawless until she blew the whistle on Garfinkel. In addition to suffering character assassination, Rennie lost her job at the university. Nils Hasselmo, the university president, announced that he stood by these decisions. However, an examination of the committee's findings by the local newspaper concluded that the "university and the corporate sponsor of the research had slanted their investigations in favor of Garfinkel."[33]

Unfortunately for Garfinkel, and fortunately for the public, the episode did not end with Garfinkel's vindication by his cronies. On February 16, 1993, Garfinkel was indicted by a federal grand jury for falsifying data in the Anafranil experiment. Six months later, a jury convicted him of five felony counts in the case, giving Rennie the vindication that she was unable to get at the university. President Hasselmo, upon hearing the verdict, issued a statement saying that "I can only imagine what a terrible ordeal this must be for Dr. Garfinkel and his family." The presidential savant said nothing about Rennie, who had been driven from her job, faced character assassination, and eventually moved from Minnesota.[34]

Corporate Culture Comes to Campus

Universities' attacks on whistleblowers, and the message that these attacks send to potential whistleblowers, can be explained in large part by universities' total engrossment in raising money. Whistleblowers might shed light on wrongdoing in the laboratory, but their actions inhibit rather than help fund raising. Because whistleblowing scares away corporate and government grant money, universities punish whistleblowers, not wrongdoers. The value of medical research at these universities is defined by how much money it brings in, not by its ultimate value to the public.

When wrongdoing is discovered in research laboratories, the first thing that such universities do is to deny it. Universities must return monies when experiments have not followed the procedures established by the grant or contract. This fear of losing grant money was clearly the motivation at the University of Pittsburgh, for example, when it discovered that scientific fraud had been perpetrated by one of its researchers, Dr. Stephen Breuning. Although the university secretly urged Breuning to resign, it publicly asserted that Breuning had not committed fraud and that it would not return Breuning's grant money to the funding source, the National Institute for Mental Health. Only after Breuning pleaded guilty to research fraud charges in federal court did the university return the $163,000 to the institute.[35]

The motivation for scientific fraud among researchers is somewhat different. In some instances, fraud is intentionally perpetrated to make money for the researcher. These flagrant cases, however, are probably fairly uncommon. More important is the overall impact of the corporate culture and its worship of success on researchers. When researchers have a financial stake in the outcome of their research, they have an incentive to err on the side of their finances, even if this is not done consciously. As Diana Zuckerman, a health policy analyst for the U.S. Senate, noted, "Many ways exist to analyze data, and if the results are not dramatic one way or the other, a scientist could be motivated to find a significant result where none really exists, to omit some potentially relevant information, or even to unintentionally skew the findings."[36] Zuckerman contends that this is most likely to occur when researchers have financial ties to companies that sponsor their research.

Some attempts to curb such abuses have certainly been made. But when the National Institutes of Health, for example, attempted to adopt guidelines in 1989 to limit conflicts of interest, the guidelines were shot down by a coalition of biotech corporations, university administrators, and biomedical professors. The proposed guidelines would have, among other things, prohibited researchers from having financial ties to "any company that would be affected by the outcome of the research." After the proposed guidelines were published, however, the NIH received an avalanche of letters opposing them.[37]

The attitudes of David Korn, vice president of the Stanford University Medical Center, and Karl Hittelman, the associate chancellor at the University of California at San Francisco, typify the comments in these letters. Korn wrote that the guidelines "will accomplish little else other than to stifle research creativity and rapid transfer of the fruits of that research to the public benefit." Hittelman indignantly wrote that an "insidious assumption...seems to underlie the guidelines: that the university biomedical research community is motivated primarily by venality and is incapable of effective self-regulation."[38]

After the NIH's conflict-of-interest guidelines were killed, some universities, particularly those racked by highly publicized scientific-fraud charges, adopted their own guidelines; but the guidelines were often weak or had loopholes. Harvard, for example, now requires its faculty to report potential conflicts of interest, but the reports are "strictly confidential." Professors at Harvard and their family members cannot own stocks in, or work as consultants to, corporations when they are conducting clinical trials on that company's products, unless they get administration approval to buy the stocks. Professors are also required to publicly disclose their financial ties to businesses in published research articles or public speeches, when the articles or speeches concern the company or its products.[39]

While these guidelines may seem like steps forward, they are really not so new. Harvard's guideline that professors disclose conflicts of interest in published articles has actually been a requirement of many biomedical journals for some time. In 1989, after the conflicts of interest of some contributors were disclosed, the *Journal of the American Medical Association* (*JAMA*) adopted a policy requiring authors to disclose all "affiliations with or involvement in any organization or entity with a direct financial interest in the subject matter described in the manuscript (e.g., employment, consultancies, stock ownership, honoraria, expert testimony)."[40]

Despite this disclosure requirement, however, not all professors on the corporate dole have been forthcoming about their financial ties. Dr. James D. Cherry, a professor of pediatrics at UCLA, wrote an editorial in *JAMA* claiming that the dangers associated with taking diphtheria-tetanus-pertussis vaccine were negligible. Cherry's editorial didn't mention that he was a consultant to one of the two manufacturers of the vaccine or that he received hundreds of thousands of dollars in research money from the same manufacturer. Only after Boston television station WHDH-TV learned about Cherry's relationship with the vaccine manufacturer—and asked him about it—did Cherry contact *JAMA* and disclose his conflict of interest. When asked about his lack of candor by a *Los Angeles Times* reporter, Cherry replied that he didn't think he needed to disclose his corporate ties because "the editorial relates in no way to a specific manufacturer, it relates to pertussis vaccine."[41]

Avarice and Vanity

According to William Broad and Nicholas Wade, the authors of *Betrayers of the Truth*, a book about scientific misconduct, the "biomedical research community" is motivated both by avarice and vanity.[42] Broad and Wade argue that scientific research is a strategy by which scientists seek financial rewards and social standing, rather than seeking the truth. University scientists, like their corporate counterparts, are motivated by careerism and the "good life" that success brings.

Broad and Wade observe that the problem is "the barrels, not the bad apples." Deliberate fraud is a symptom of the problems with biomedical research, but it is not the major problem. The major problem is that university culture emphasizes economic and social advancement over knowledge. Professors who get grants and publish grant-funded research articles are rewarded by their universities. They get travel funds to attend conferences at popular resort areas, reduced teaching responsibilities, big salaries, and high-status appointments.

To qualify for these perks, professors must get their publications out quickly. This is the motivation that leads someone like Dr. Barry Garfinkel to commit fraud. Other professors who conduct less research and publish fewer papers can get the same perks and income by going outside the university—that is, by becoming corporate consultants and stockholders. These professorial representatives of industry also get travel funds and other perks from their corporate sponsors. Still other professors, such as those at the University of Minnesota's medical school, get their perks and income by operating private practices out of their university offices.[43]

The motivations of these biomedical researchers reflect the motivations of the university and its administrators. Administrators have shown their faculties what they consider to be important, and professors have followed their example. This has tremendously benefited administrators, many professors, and corporations—but it has not been a boon to the public.

Chapter Four

Nobody's Business but Their Own: The Business of Business Schools

Long before academicians in the sciences became entrepreneurs, professors in business departments had given up teaching for more lucrative pursuits—while still collecting their university salaries. In the late 1970s and early 1980s, many business professors signed on as corporate consultants, started their own businesses, did research for corporate clients (which they later published as though it were research done to expand the frontiers of knowledge, rather than their bank accounts), or became for-hire "experts," who testify on behalf of corporations during trials and government inquiries.

One of these entrepreneurial pioneers is Russell Haley, who recently retired from the University of New Hampshire. For about 15 years, Professor Haley operated a consulting firm named Russ Haley & Associates, which provided marketing advice to business clients.[1] For most of those years, he ran the company while working as a professor at New Hampshire.

Other business professors have followed in Haley's footsteps, and some have outstripped his entrepreneurship. For example, Thomas J. Reynolds, a professor of marketing at the University of Texas at Dallas, also "serves as chairman of Strategic Assessment, Inc. and as managing director of Richmont Partners, a private merchant bank."[2] If Reynolds put in just seven hours a day at each of his jobs, he would get three hours of sleep each night, provided that he didn't take time to shave, shower, eat, or brush his teeth. As another example, Harvard business professor Michael Porter is a cofounder and director of the Monitor Co., a management consulting firm. While Haley's company has just a few employees, Monitor has a staff of 200 and annual revenues of $30 million. Porter, who served as an appointee to President Reagan's Commission on Industrial Competitiveness, has AT&T, Westinghouse, and other corporate giants as clients.[3]

The interest that professors like these have exhibited in starting businesses, working as consultants, or testifying as experts has created a new industry akin to the dating services that advertise in singles magazines. This industry matches up professors seeking corporate ties with corporations seeking professorial expertise. For example, North American BEST, a computer database, sells information on professors' research interests, universities' research facilities, university patents and inventions, and even graduate students' backgrounds. Corporations seeking a university that will conduct their research or a professor to consult for them can retrieve the information from BEST's computer for an annual fee ranging from $8,500 to $25,000. As of 1991, BEST had information in its computers on 90 universities, and its owners were hoping to add information on another 30. BEST is owned by Cartermill, Inc. and headed by Kenneth Blaisdell, a former Johns Hopkins University administrator. Cartermill is partly owned by Johns Hopkins's for-profit company, the Dome Corporation.[4]

Another professor-corporate liaison company is the Technical Advisory Service for Attorneys (TAS), which often advertises for "experts" in higher-education periodicals. In its advertising, directed at attorneys, it uses the slogan, "The single source for all your expert needs." TAS maintains a roster of professors in many disciplines who will appear in court as "expert witnesses" for attorneys. The service claims to have 9,600 experts in 3,700 categories who are willing to testify about anything, if the price is right. University of Michigan business professor Claude Martin, who worked for TAS as an expert witness, reported that the company charges attorneys a fee for each day that an academic "expert" is preparing for trial or appearing in court.

Professor Martin appeared as an "expert witness" on advertising and consumer behavior for tobacco companies in a suit in which Antonio Cipollone sued Philip Morris, Lorillard, and the Liggett Group for causing the death of his wife, Rose. (Rose Cipollone died of lung cancer after smoking more than a pack of cigarettes a day for 40 years. Before dying, Rose signed a deposition stating that she had continued to smoke because she believed cigarette advertising, which portrayed smoking as safe.[5])

Both Martin and TAS were well-compensated for their participation in the suit. Martin received $1,800 a day while preparing for the Cipollone trial. TAS received $360 per day. During court appearances, Martin was paid $2,700 a day, during which TAS received $450. Overall, Martin pocketed more than $74,000 for his testimony, a dandy supplement to his university salary. (During the 1993-94 academic year, Martin's salary was $100,000.)

During the trial, Martin testified that tobacco companies spend millions of dollars on advertising because "they are afraid not to." He asserted that cigarette advertising and public relations campaigns are a "relatively small component of the information environment" and do not entice people to smoke. Martin insisted that the advertisements promoted nothing more than brand switching among current smokers. Presiding Judge H. Lee Sarokin apparently found Martin's testimony so hard to believe that he took the unusual step of directly questioning him:

> Judge Sarokin: Doesn't that depend upon the content of the advertising and public relations?
> Claude Martin: There is no way of saying, here's some content and this is the effect that it is going to have.
> Judge Sarokin: If a cigarette manufacturer put out an ad showing an attractive young woman in a tennis outfit in a nice setting, or put an ad for a funeral for that woman and said, "Smoking kills," you mean that second ad would not have an impact upon the information environment?
> Claude Martin: Well, first of all, I think we've stepped over the line because you've already [specified that] we have an attractive young woman. I've seen some advertisements that some people who might be younger in this courtroom would think are attractive people, I might look at them and think they're not attractive. It's as the old saying goes, "It's only in the eyes of the beholder."

Sarokin stated that he found Martin's answer unresponsive, and rephrased his question, saying he was "trying to find out if it's your opinion that if a tobacco company acknowledges the dangers of smoking and sets that forth in public relations or advertising, that would have no impact on the information environment?"

"It could have an impact, but again we come to source credibility," Martin responded.[6]

After having testified as an expert witness for the tobacco companies, Martin started publishing articles critical of research finding a link between advertising and smoking initiation.[7] His articles on tobacco advertising were published by the *Journal of Advertising,* the American Statistical Association, the American Association of Public Opinion Research, and the Association for Consumer Research. The *Journal of Advertising* article typifies his writings. It criticizes a research study reported in the *Journal of the American Medical Association*, which showed that Camel cigarette's Joe Camel character is as well-known among children as Mickey Mouse. Martin never mentions in the article that he had received tobacco company money.[8]

Professor Martin is just one of many business school professors who have supplemented their incomes by serving as experts on tobacco advertising. Like Martin, most of these "experts" do not disclose their financial arrangements in published biographies, testimonies, or published research articles about cigarette advertising. For example, University of Pennsylvania business professor Scott Ward, who has frequently testified about the effects of cigarette advertising on behalf of the tobacco industry in congressional hearings, published a report in the *International Journal of Advertising* which concluded that "advertising plays a negligible role in smoking initiation or maintenance," but never mentioned in it his work for the tobacco companies.[9] The article concluded that children are "street-wise" and not affected by tobacco advertising. Ward based his conclusion on "experiments" that he conducted on children over a 20-year period.

During congressional hearings on tobacco advertising that were conducted during the late 1980s and early 1990s, Ward was a ubiquitous witness for the tobacco companies. Like Claude Martin, he testified that cigarette advertising promoted brand switching among smokers but did not induce young people to smoke. "The role of advertising for mature markets [like cigarettes] is to keep consumers who use the product loyal to the brand being advertised or to prompt consumers of other brands to switch," Ward testified.[10]

Ward's extracurricular activities, such as providing expert testimony in favor of the tobacco industry, must have been lucrative, because he purchased a 16-room mansion surrounded by a ten-foot-high brick wall for $550,000 in 1984, according to the *Philadelphia Inquirer*. The mansion was described in news reports of Ward's arrest for statutory rape and corruption of minors.[11]

Ward might be the only professor on the tobacco-company dole who has been charged with corrupting minors, but he is not the only professor who has failed to divulge tobacco-industry ties when writing articles about cigarette advertising. Florida State University marketing professor Richard Mizerski was hired by R.J. Reynolds to rebut research published in the *Journal of the American Medical Association*, which showed that R.J. Reynolds's Joe Camel character was targeting children. Needless to say, Mizerski issued a report claiming that the *JAMA* research was flawed. After Mizerski's report was released, he was asked by the American Medical Association how much R.J. Reynolds had paid him for his work. Mizerski refused to disclose the amount.[12] He also didn't disclose that he was on the tobacco-company payroll in a published synopsis of his findings in the *Proceedings of the 1993 Conference of the American Academy of Advertising*. The report, which claimed that the *JAMA* articles were "conceptually and methodologically flawed," mentioned only Mizerski's university affiliation.[13]

Another business school savant who testified for the tobacco industry during congressional hearings is Roger Blackwell, a professor at Ohio State University in Columbus, who testified that no "research suggests that advertising influences children to view smoking in a positive light...To the contrary, the research that is available revealed in young people a skepticism and distaste for cigarette advertising."[14] In addition to testifying on behalf of the cancer industry and working as a professor, Blackwell has managed to find time to be president of Roger Blackwell Associates, Inc., a consulting firm.

Consulting

Blackwell, in fact, is only one of a huge number of business professors who operate consulting businesses. Moonlighting is discouraged in most occupations—but not in academia, where it is politely described as "consulting." "At all good business schools, at least half the faculty is doing consulting," reports University of Nevada at Reno business professor Robert Metzger, who has written two textbooks on consulting.[15]

Many university administrators encourage their business professors to work for corporations when they're not in the classroom. "It helps professors keep in touch with the business world," says an administrator at the City University of New York's Baruch College, where professors frequently supplement their teaching incomes with consulting. Darrell R. Lewis, an administrator at the University of Minnesota, co-authored a report suggesting that professors should "not only be permitted but encouraged" to continue their consulting. Lewis claims that limitations on academic moonlighting may restrict "the productivity of highly active faculty."[16]

By "productivity," Lewis means the publishing of scholarly articles. He suggests that professors who consult are more likely to publish than those who do not—and he is right. Professors who consult frequently publish articles based on their consulting, but they also often fail to mention in the articles that the research was done for some corporate client. This has allowed corporations to covertly influence the content and direction of scholarly research.

To encourage such "productivity," most universities have policies that allow professors to consult at least one day per week, or up to one-fifth of their time. This is far more time than most professors devote to research. Indeed, a congressional subcommittee report on universities found that "more than half of all professors devote fewer than 5 hours a week to research."[17]

Consulting by business professors isn't designed to keep them out of poverty. Even without their consulting dollars, business professors are well paid compared to professors of English, languages, history, or fine arts. At Michigan State University, the average salary of assistant professors of accounting, which is the entry-level professorial rank, was $67,050 for the 1993-94 academic year. Full professors averaged $89,750. Assistant professors of marketing, one of the lowest-paid fields in business schools, averaged $57,000. Full professors averaged $88,350.[18]

The salaries of business school professors at most large institutions are similar to those at Michigan State. For example, the

University of Wisconsin at Madison pays assistant professors of accounting an average of $72,533, assistant professors of finance an average of $71,108, and assistant professors of marketing an average of $63,140. Full professors of marketing averaged $92,717 during 1993-94. By contrast, the average salaries of assistant professors of some humanities were as follows: $33,767 for comparative literature, $35,423 for art history, and $34,825 for East Asian languages and literature. The salaries of full professors of East Asian languages and literature averaged $50,670.[19]

At more prestigious institutions, such as Harvard and Stanford, business professors are paid even more and command notoriously high consulting fees. For example, when Harvard finance professors Robert R. Glauber and David W. Mullins, Jr. accepted appointments in President Bush's Treasury Department in 1989, they were required to disclose their personal finances. In 1988, Glauber had noninvestment income of $874,445, of which $120,00 was his Harvard salary. Consulting fees accounted for $515,750. Glauber's clients included Morgan Guaranty Trust Co., Aetna Life Insurance, Excel Insurance Co., Dreyfus Funds, Dillon Read & Co., Circuit City Stores, Quantum Chemical Co., Avon Products, and Sunbelt Coca-Cola Bottling Co. He made an additional $100,000 or so from capital gains, dividends, and interest. According to the disclosure form, Glauber, who has spent his academic life at Harvard, had assets of around $2 million.[20] Professor Mullins's noninvestment income in 1988 was a "meager" $347,969. The majority of it also came from consulting.[21]

Although professors and university administrators describe consulting as a benign method for professors to make a few dollars on the side, a different view is presented by Richard Pollay, a marketing professor at the University of British Columbia. Pollay says that money received from companies or industries for consulting and research influences academia "all the way through the system—with working papers, conference papers, and journal articles." He also says that when companies "throw their money into universities, it's like throwing fertilizer and water on a lawn—the money leads to a growth of friendly research." Moreover, according to Pollay, "Professors who are funded by industries like the tobacco industry have money to travel to conferences, to do research, to get it published, and the industries make sure that views friendly to them get circulated. Views that aren't friendly to industry don't get funded."[22]

There is ample evidence to support Pollay's statements. After Professor Ward testified on behalf of the tobacco industry during 1989 congressional hearings, the Tobacco Institute sent out a press release describing his testimony.[23] The Tobacco Institute also sent a copy of Professor Ward's testimony to *The Quill*, the magazine of the Society of Professional Journalists, when the magazine wanted a statement opposing tobacco advertising restrictions.[24]

It isn't just the tobacco industry that hires professors to influence Congress and regulators—many other industries do as well. AT&T has hired numerous economists and social scientists as consultants. A study by University of Pennsylvania professor Edward Herman found that AT&T made "payments to 104 named social scientists and 215 small consulting firms, many associated with academicians" between 1978 and 1980.[25] In 1981, AT&T paid $3.5 million to professors and academic consultants, who performed research for the company or testified on its behalf during federal, state, and local commission hearings. Several Stanford University economists were given huge payments by AT&T that year: Professor Nathan Rosenberg received $82,672, Professor Kenneth Arrow received $41,775, and Professors James Rosse and Ray Olszewski split a whopping $241,629.[26]

Another professor who worked as a telephone industry consultant is marketing professor Jagdish Sheth, currently at Emory University in Atlanta, Georgia. In 1981, his consulting firm, Sheth Associates, Inc., received $115,042 from AT&T.[27] He has received varying amounts from telephone companies since then. Like his cohorts who work for the tobacco industry, Sheth writes articles that favor the positions of his corporate sponsors while failing to disclose his corporate ties. For example, Sheth published an op-ed article in the *Chicago Tribune* in 1991 entitled "Caller ID Benefits Outweigh Perils" to laud the benefits of caller ID technology, which Illinois Bell was trying to get the Illinois utility commission to approve. Sheth described himself in the op-ed byline as "the founder of the Center for Telecommunications Management at the University of

Southern California," with which he was affiliated at the time, rather than as a telephone-company consultant.[28]

An astute reader of Sheth's op-ed article wrote a letter to the *Tribune*'s editor, observing that Sheth's position "seems consistent with that taken by Illinois Bell in their current proposal before the Illinois Commerce Commission to offer ID service in Illinois." The reader added that he had attended a seminar a year earlier, where Professor Sheth admitted that "he (or one of his companies) had performed consulting work for...Ameritech, Illinois Bell's parent company." The letter closed with the following paragraph:

> I find it disturbing that no mention was made in his column of his past (or, perhaps, present) affiliation with an organization that stands to benefit from the action he is recommending. Had your readers been informed of his association with Ameritech, they could have decided for themselves whether his recommendation resulted from an academic's impartial review...or a consultant's desire to enhance his posture with a large corporate client for a current or future business relationship.[29]

When business school professors are not publishing articles promoting the agendas of their corporate clients, they are pumping out reams of "scholarly research" articles with impressive-sounding titles such as "The Relationship between Prior Brand Knowledge Acquisition and Information Order Acquisition," "The Differential Processing of Product Category and Noncomparable Choice Alternatives," and "Alternative Approaches to Understanding the Determinants of Typicality."[30]

Although impressively titled, such articles are full of "jargon, obfuscating convolutions and nebulous verbosity...[the] verbiage increases to the extent that ambition exceeds knowledge," as author and university critic Charles Sykes has noted.[31]

In fact, a 1988 study sponsored by the American Assembly of Collegiate Schools of Business, the accrediting organization for college business programs, concluded that the impact of business professors' academic research is "virtually nil." The report continues, "The business world is not very aware of what research is being carried out, and when managers and executives are aware of what research is being carried out, they typically report that they do not pay much attention to it." The report also concluded that much business school research was "trivial and irrelevant."[32]

Despite the irrelevance and unreadability of this academic research, there is a growing, rather than shrinking, number of journals in which business school professors publish their profundities. In marketing alone, there are over two dozen "scholarly" journals, including *Journal of Public Policy and Marketing, Journal of Consumer Research,* and *International Journal of Research in Marketing* (see sidebar).

If you think that it's prestigious to have an article in an international research journal such as the *International Journal of Research in Marketing,* you're wrong. The journal has an international circulation of only 800, and almost all copies are sold to libraries at an annual subscription rate of $253—for a mere four issues. Some of these journals have even smaller circulations. The *Journal of Hospital Marketing,* for example, has a circulation of 237, and a subscription to it costs $120. Classified ads in Scooba, Mississippi's weekly newspaper are more widely read. Moreover, the authors of articles in these journals aren't paid a nickel for their contributions. The articles' main value is to pad the résumés of their authors and to provide an excuse for business professors to give up teaching. "I'm too busy doing research," is the usual explanation given by business professors who have abandoned the classroom.

Although the articles in these journals are irrelevant, libraries subscribe to them at the urging of professors, who like to see their names in print. Naturally, the subscription costs are paid by students and taxpayers, whose tuition and tax dollars are used to subsidize this ego gratification.

Chambers of Commerce

In order to find time for consulting, running their companies, or producing the wisdom contained in "scholarly" articles, professors at business schools have drastically reduced the amount of time they spend teaching. At some institutions, business professors teach just six months each year, leaving half the year for consulting or conducting "research" (which is often synonymous with consulting). And at many universities, business professors teach just two classes, or six hours, per week. On average, business professors teach far less than their colleagues in the humanities but get much higher salaries, which they then supplement with corporate dollars.

One of biggest scams used by business school professors to escape from teaching is the publishing of "scholarly research articles." Professors who publish "research articles" invariably get reduced teaching responsibilities, and this reduction gives them free time to do additional consulting. But the general public does not realize that there is an endless number of such journals, many of which have circulations only in the hundreds. None pay the authors for the articles; some charge the authors "page proof fees," making them little more than vanity presses.

There are innumerable journals for professors of economics, finance, management, accounting, and marketing to publish in. Below is a partial list of the journals that professors of marketing use to pad their résumés and escape from teaching.

Current Issues and Research in Advertising
Health Marketing Quarterly
Industrial Marketing Management
International Journal of Research in Marketing
International Journal of Advertising
Journal of Advertising
Journal of Advertising Research
Journal of Business and Industrial Marketing
Journal of Business Logistics
Journal of Business-to-Business Marketing
Journal of Consumer Marketing
Journal of Consumer Research
Journal of Direct Marketing
Journal of Euromarketing
Journal of Food Products Marketing
Journal of Hospital Marketing
Journal of International Consumer Marketing
Journal of International Marketing
Journal of International Marketing & Marketing Research
Journal of Macromarketing
Journal of Marketing
Journal of Marketing Channels
Journal of Marketing Education
Journal of Marketing for Higher Education
Journal of Marketing Management
Journal of Marketing Research
Journal of Promotion Management
Journal of Public Policy and Marketing
Journal of Retailing
Journal of Strategic Marketing

University administrators tolerate, and even support, this situation because business-faculty ties with corporations are a form of "university-industry interaction," which administrators promote.

This promotion can go to great lengths. In order to reduce the teaching load of business school professors, some universities have even cut the budgets of other departments, particularly the humanities and social sciences. This is what occurred at the University of Minnesota. In 1991, Minnesota hired David S. Kidwell as dean of the university's business school. The university offered Kidwell an annual salary of $196,000 and guaranteed him an additional $29,000 in business consulting fees. The university also promised Kidwell that it would try to get him named to the board of directors of a Twin Cities corporation and give him up to $17,000 in moving expenses—enough to literally move his home to Minnesota from Connecticut, where he then lived. At the time that Kidwell was hired, the university promised him that it would spend $40-$45 million for a new business school building, an additional $1.5 million in funds for the school's operation and maintenance budget, and enough money to hire six new business professors.

However, while the university was making these promises, it was also scaling back funding for other parts of the university, particularly language and regional studies programs. According to a letter sent to Kidwell by university provost Leonard Kuhi, part of the money for the business school was to come at the expense of other university programs, which had already been cut back. Kuhi informed Kidwell that the new money for the business school "will require retrenchment of other programs *in addition to* the $31.9 million reductions that we have presented to our board [of regents], and $20 million of programmatic retrenchments previously scheduled."[33]

In a now familiar scenario, while the University of Minnesota was pouring more money into its business school, the amount of time that its business school professors spent teaching was actually shrinking. One alienated professor at Minnesota's business school, who believed that teaching was the university's main mission, complained in 1991 that administrators lied to the public about the teaching requirements of business professors. "The publicly stated teaching load is five classes [per year], but that's not what people teach," the professor asserted.[34] The actual teaching schedule for most professors is three classes, which means that the typical marketing professor teaches three hours per week during one quarter, six hours per week during another, and has six months free, during which he or she can work full-time on consulting or running a business.

The 1990-91 class schedule published by the University of Minnesota supports the charges leveled by that dissident professor. The schedule shows that faculty in the marketing and logistics management department taught only six months a year. They taught a maximum of three classes; some taught fewer than that. Nevertheless, the chairman of the marketing department publicly maintained that "the modal teaching load for the department is five classes."[35]

Such diminutive teaching requirements, particularly for professors in business schools, have helped push up tuition rates at a pace far faster than the rate of inflation. Tuition rates have increased nearly 7 percent annually during the past decade. At many universities, annual tuition rates at business schools are now higher than at law schools, which are more expensive to operate because they require a separate law library, publish a law review, and require high-tech equipment for accessing computer databases such as Lexis and Westlaw. (Law school professors' salaries are also high, and many do consulting, but not nearly as much as business school professors.) The top five law schools in the United States, as ranked by *U.S. News & World Report*,[36] charged less for tuition than did business schools at the same universities:

	Business School Annual Tuition	Law School Annual Tuition
Law School Ranking		
1. Yale	$20,220	$18,548
2. Harvard	$19,750	$17,750
3. Stanford	$20,196	$20,186
4. Chicago	$20,200	$19,095
5. Columbia	$20,050	$20,000

The high, and steadily increasing, tuition charged by universities means that students (and taxpayers at public universities) are subsidizing the consulting, expert testimony, and businesses that professors operate. These tuition increases are used to pay the salaries of newly hired professors who teach the courses that other professors would have taught, if the latter had not abandoned the classroom for consulting.

At universities (such as the University of Minnesota) that have transferred funding from liberal arts departments to business schools, liberal arts students are also, through these transfers, subsidizing the consulting and businesses of business school professors. But, in return, they are getting a substandard education. In another example similar to Minnesota, at the University of Wisconsin at Madison dance and fine arts courses are taught in Lathrop Hall, an 83-year-old building that does not meet fire codes. The basement contains asbestos and the heating system is an antiquated propeller-driven device. Since 1971, the education college, in which the arts and dance programs are located, has sought $3.1 million to renovate Lathrop Hall. For over 20 years, they have failed to get the money.

In contrast, the university built a $40 million, state-of-the-art facility called Grainger Hall for the business school. According to the *Milwaukee Journal*, Grainger and Lathrop halls "represent the haves and have-nots in the academic world."[37] Grainger Hall was built because corporations and industrialists were willing to contribute 30 percent of the construction costs, leaving taxpayers to pick up "just" 70 percent, or $28 million. Because the dance program doesn't have any wealthy patrons, its students have been forced to accept their substandard facilities.

Monuments to Moguls

In addition to illustrating the discrepancy between the humanities and business schools, the University of Wisconsin case contains an example of another widespread trend. Eight million dollars of the private contributions to the Wisconsin business school's building fund came from a single individual, David W. Grainger, and his Grainger Foundation, for which the building is now named. Grainger owns W. W. Grainger, a giant industrial distributorship.

And Grainger is not the only industrialist who has contributed to his or her favorite business school or had his or her name attached to an edifice, statue, or even a whole school. Michigan State University has the Eli Broad College of Business and Eli Broad

Graduate School of Management, both named for an alumnus and financier who in 1991 promised to give the business school $20 million.[38] Like the University of Wisconsin, Michigan State is constructing a new building to house its *nouveau riche* business school. The business school, in an effort to raise even more money, is seeking contributions from every corporation and tycoon in Michigan, and naming every floor and office of its new building for these contributors. The second floor of the building is named after the Kresge Foundation, a 350-seat lecture hall is named for the Ford Motor Company, the fourth floor is named for a Toyota dealer, the fifth floor is named for the Chrysler Corporation, and the MBA lounge is named for the First of Michigan Corp.[39] When finished, the business school building will contain more advertising than an issue of *Cosmopolitan* magazine.

Between 1980 and 1990, most large universities named their business schools for tycoons who contributed large sums of money to them. Rather than giving the money and bowing out, however, many of the fat-cat contributors have exercised a "hands-on" policy toward the recipients of their "largesse." At Michigan State, for example, millionaire donor Eli Broad threatened to cut off funding if the university did not appoint a business school dean of his liking. The candidates being considered for the post had too much academic experience and too little hands-on business experience, Broad contended.[40]

New York University and the University of Rochester provide other examples of tycoon influence. NYU has the Leonard N. Stern School of Business, named after the chairman of the Hartz Group, who gave the school $30 million in 1988. Stern is a member of NYU's board of trustees, which sets the policies and direction of the university.[41] The University of Rochester in Rochester, New York has the William E. Simon School of Business, named after a former Nixon administration official and archconservative who is the business school's ideological mentor. He contributed $15 million to the school in 1986. Like Stern, he sits on the university's board of trustees.[42]

In a variation on individual tycoon donations, some business schools have also raised cash by opening "centers" that cultivate good relations with one specific industry; this industry, in turn, donates money to the business school. Still other business schools have made deals with individual corporations to bring in cash. In either case, the corporate contributions are tax-deductible because university business schools are nonprofit, tax-exempt institutions.

Typical of such centers is the A.C. Nielsen Center for Marketing Research at the University of Wisconsin at Madison. The center is named for marketing research mogul A. C. Nielsen, whose heirs donated $4 million to get it up and running. The center describes itself as being in a "partnership with business" and has an advisory board of executives from AT&T, Coca-Cola, Helene Curtis, General Motors, Goodyear Tire & Rubber, McDonald's, Miller Brewing, and Ralston Purina.[43]

The purpose of the center is "scholarly work and the preparation of graduate students"—in that order, according to the center's literature.[44] "Scholarly work" is defined as "efficient experimental methods to link sales and marketing activities," "demographic systems to establish market potentials," and a host of other activities designed to benefit businesses, not the public.[45] This "research" is used to justify the high salaries and limited teaching responsibilities of its professors.

The center's graduate program "admits 10 to 20 students per year," which explains why the teaching requirements of professors associated with the center are minuscule.[46] Its director received a salary of $120,095 for teaching just one course each semester, which amounts to two and a half hours per week of teaching.[47] When a representative in the associate dean's office was asked about this, she replied that "it's not unusual for an instructor not to teach, especially for someone [who] teaches graduate courses. That's because they're doing research."[48]

The director of the A.C. Nielsen Center explained his one-class-per-semester teaching responsibilities this way: "I buy out my time." When asked to clarify what this meant, he stated that "I pay back the dean and then the dean uses the money to hire someone to teach the class."[49] The "adjunct professors" that deans typically hire from such "buy-out" money are paid just a few thousand dollars for teaching each course, instead of the six-figure salaries that full-professors of business (like the head of the A.C. Nielsen Center) get paid. Adjunct professors are not only paid little for what they do, but they also usually receive the same benefits as an hourly worker at McDonald's—that is, none. In the *Washington Post*, columnist

Colman McCarthy described these adjunct professors as "academia's stoop laborers."[50]

Not only are adjunct professors short-changed, but so are the students who take their courses. Because adjunct professors cannot live on what they are paid for teaching, they must make their living another way, and therefore spend little time on campus, have little time available for meeting with students, and often pay far less attention to classroom preparation than they should. In Los Angeles, adjunct professors are described as "freeway fliers" by their full-time colleagues because they rush from one job to another.

The Nielsen Center and its teaching arrangements are far from unique. The Anderson School of Business at UCLA, for example, has a half-dozen centers with names such as the Center for Finance and Real Estate, Center for Technology Management, Entrepreneurial Studies Center, and the John M. Olin Center for Public Policy. The Olin Center is associated with a number of right-wing think tanks, including the Washington-based American Enterprise Institute, with which it co-sponsored a 1993 conference on the UCLA campus (see Chapter Seven for a discussion of off- and on-campus right-wing think tanks). The Olin Center's director received a salary of $97,000 during the 1993-94 school year, but, according to UCLA's *Schedule of Classes*, taught just one course per term.[51] When asked about his diminutive teaching schedule in a telephone interview, the Olin Center director explained that his teaching responsibilities were reduced because of his "administrative responsibilities."[52]

The University of Michigan business school operates a similar center, the William Davidson Institute, which is dedicated to bringing capitalism to Eastern Europe. The center is funded by William Davidson, the chairman of the board of Guardian Industries, which does business in Eastern Europe and Asia.[53]

Michigan's business school also contracted with Cathay Pacific Airways to teach courses and grant MBAs to Cathay's employees in Hong Kong, who will take courses through satellite video-conferencing. Assignments will be handed out and collected via computer networks and fax machines.[54] B. Joseph White, dean of Michigan's business school, explained to *Business Week* why his school entered into the agreement with Cathay Pacific. White said, "We are all striving to increase our international visibility, enhance international faculty development—and everybody is looking for attractive financial opportunities."[55] Professor White is correct. Business schools and their professors are always "looking for attractive financial opportunities"—at students' and taxpayers' expense.

 Chapter Five

The Unsocial Sciences

Psychology and sociology evolved into disciplines in the late 19th century when the principles of empiricism were applied to the study of the human mind and society. But by the mid-20th century, the social sciences had become instruments at the disposal of nation states. In the Soviet Union, Marxism was elevated from social scientific paradigm to state creed. In Germany, social scientists worked to further the aims of the Third Reich. And in the United States during World War II, the Office of War Information, the Office of Strategic Services, and other government agencies enlisted the services of social scientists to combat the Third Reich.

When the war ended, many U.S. social scientists resigned from their government posts but continued to work covertly for the government. Political scientist Evron Kirkpatrick, a veteran of the Office of Strategic Services, left the State Department in 1954 to become executive director of the American Political Science Association, the leading academic organization in the field. In 1955, Kirkpatrick became head of Operations and Policy Research, Inc., an ostensibly private company that was actually a CIA conduit.[1] Other political scientists and historians followed in Kirkpatrick's footsteps.[2]

In the early Cold War era, much of the social science research produced at universities, and published in prominent research journals such as *Public Opinion Quarterly*, was "prepared under government contract—though not publicly acknowledged as such."[3] Through covert funding and political pressures, the U.S. government dominated much of the social scientific thinking of the early Cold War era.[4]

By the 1980s, many social scientists had severed their government ties for far more lucrative relationships with corporations. Professors in psychology, sociology, and other fields turned to consulting, expert testimony, and other sources of supplemental income, just as professors in business and medicine have (see Chapters Three and Four). Like the post-World War II professors, many of these contemporary social scientists publish "scholarly articles" based on their work for corporations but do not acknowledge their sources of funding.

The incentives for these professors to moonlight for corporations are not difficult to determine. Social scientists receive relatively small salaries compared to medical, engineering, and business professors, and park their Volvos and Hondas in university parking lots next to the BMW convertibles and Mercedes Benzes owned by their higher-paid colleagues. According to a 1994 study of the College and University Personnel Association, the average starting salary for assistant professors of anthropology, communication, history, political science, and sociology was $32,800 a year. In these disciplines, the average salary of full professors, the highest academic rank, was $55,700. In contrast, as mentioned in a previous chapter, the average salary of assistant professors of anesthesiology (a middle-income medical specialization) was $147,800 in 1991.[5]

Consulting jobs from corporations can provide social scientists with far more money than their professorships. These potential financial rewards explain why social science professors find corporate relationships so desirable. For instance, the average pay of independent consultants who work for corporations is $800-$1,000 per day, although some make as "little" as $400 per day. Others make considerably more.[6]

Such corporate consulting can so blur the distinction between university employment and corporate freelance work that the two are nearly indistinguishable—even in the mind of the consultant. At a 1994 academic conference in Tucson, a University of Kentucky communications professor, who described research he did for DuPont during a paper presentation, said that DuPont "pays our salaries." After pausing a moment, the professor clarified his statement, saying, "At least they pay a portion of it. They pay more than the university pays."[7]

The paper that this communications professor discussed, like much published social science research, presented findings that were based on a consulting project. Specifically, the study described a research technique used to evaluate advertisements for a new agricultural herbicide. The paper presented research commissioned by DuPont, but just "selected aspects" of it—those parts that DuPont permitted the researchers to disclose. Other parts were not made public, and when asked to clarify an issue during the paper presentation, the professor said that he could not because "DuPont doesn't want us to talk about it."[8]

The Impact of Consulting

One of the quickest routes to higher income for social scientists has been to change the focus of their research from socially significant issues—such as the causes of poverty—for which there is little monetary reward, to issues of interest to business—such as how to motivate workers to be more productive. Doing such business-related research can lead to lucrative consulting contracts and even high-paid professorial appointments.

For example, Rosabeth Moss Kanter began her studies as a sociologist with a dissertation on 19th-century utopian communes; but she abandoned this for business research because, as her husband, Barry Stein, noted, "she liked business and people pay you for it."[9] After abandoning research on communes for research on corporate management techniques, Kanter received a joint appointment in sociology and management at Yale University. One of her books on corporate management techniques, *The Change Masters: Innovation for Productivity in the American Corporation*, attracted the attention of Fortune 500 managers, and she soon became a consultant and speaker on the corporate circuit.

With her husband, Kanter started a management consulting firm, Goodmeasure, Inc., whose client list includes Honeywell, IBM, and Xerox. With an influential client list and a reputation as a much-sought-after corporate management guru, she was hired by the Harvard Business School in 1986, named editor of the *Harvard*

Business Review in 1989, and thereafter relieved of her teaching responsibilities.[10]

Purdue psychology professor Jacob Jacoby presents another example. Jacoby began his career examining issues such as open- and closed-mindedness and anxiety,[11] but he soon turned his research attention to consumer purchase behavior, an issue of importance to businesses. Jacoby left Purdue and psychology for an endowed marketing professorship, the Merchants Council Professorship of Retailing, at New York University's Stern School of Business. He has also become a consultant to DuPont, General Motors, General Electric, Standard Oil, Procter & Gamble, and various government agencies.[12]

Despite the pervasive influence of corporate consulting demonstrated in the careers of Professors Kanter and Jacoby, not all social scientists are pro-business. But even when research is critical of corporate practices, it can be easily co-opted by consulting contracts (see sidebar on multicultural research). As noted in *The Regulation Game*, a textbook written for law students and managers of regulated industries such as utility services, academicians can be easily co-opted. The book suggests that firms "should be prepared whenever possible to coopt these experts. This is most effectively done by identifying the leading experts in each relevant field and hiring them as consultants or advisors, or giving them research grants or the like. This activity requires a modicum of finesse...for the experts themselves must not recognize that they have lost their objectivity."[13] The book was written by Northwestern University professor Ronald Braeutigam and Bruce Owen, head of Duke University's Center for the Study of Regulation and Private Enterprise, an industry-supported center. Before going to Duke in Durham, North Carolina, Owen was a fellow at the Hoover Institution, Stanford's conservative think tank, and the Brookings Institution, a Washington think tank (see Chapter Seven). Owen eventually left Duke to become a full-time consultant.

More often than not, however, corporations can find willing partners in academia to work for them. As another example, George R. Packard, dean of the Paul H. Nitze School of Advanced International Studies at Johns Hopkins University and director of its Center for East Asian Studies, is a consultant to KRC Pacific Partners,

New Directions in Multicultural Research

Corporate co-optation of social science research is exemplified by multicultural research, which corporate interests initially and derisively dismissed as a form of "political correctness." However, many corporations have in recent years taken an interest in multiculturalism and the professors who are experts in it. This new interest has changed the direction and focus of such research.

In response to lawsuits charging racial and sexual harassment in the workplace, corporations have been hiring "multicultural consultants"—many of whom are professors—who conduct the corporation's diversity-training sessions. These sessions are supposed to make the workplace more hospitable to women and persons of color.

According to the *New York Times*, diversity training is one of the fastest growing industries in the United States, and consultants from a host of disciplines—including psychology, anthropology, sociology, education, and management—have started diversity-training firms.[14] The professorial consultants come from large and small, prestigious and little-known universities. For example, Vanderbilt University psychology professor Patricia Arnold operates Patricia Arnold Associates, which conducts "presentations, seminars and workshops on managing diversity, building diverse teams, [and] integrating women and minorities into the workplace" for Fortune 500 companies. University of Michigan professor of organizational behavior Taylor Cox operates Taylor Cox Associates, "which specializes in human resource work with diverse workgroups." And Derald Wing Sue, a professor in the Department of Educational Psychology at Cal State University at Hayward, is president of Cultural Diversity Training.[15]

As a result of professors having become diversity consultants, multicultural academic research has begun to focus on the best techniques to use for diversity training, rather than on such topics as the relationship between the concentration of wealth in the United States and poverty, or the relationship between poverty and racism. Social science research articles with titles such as "A Model for Cultural Diversity Training" are beginning to outnumber studies of the institutional bases of racism.

Ltd., a firm that advises Japanese companies on investing in the United States and U.S. companies on investing in Japan. Packard has even tried his hand at writing advertising copy for clients, having penned a 16-page advertisement for the Japanese Chamber of Commerce that appeared in *The Atlantic* magazine. The advertisement, titled "The U.S. and Japan: Partners in Prosperity," extolled the merits of Japan-U.S. trade and the need for more "power sharing" with Japan.[16] Packard reports that his views aren't influenced by Japanese money, but he nevertheless advocates policies that benefit Japan—policies that other academicians who have served as consultants to Japan also advocate.

Indeed, so frequently have Japanese-funded scholars taken positions consistent with Japanese government positions that *Time* magazine in its October 1, 1990 issue parodied the situation. The parody, which is based on Pat Choate's book, *Agents of Influence*, begins when a trade dispute with Japan becomes public in newspaper reports. After that, the "Japan expert" may write an op-ed piece or give an interview supporting the Japanese position and attacking Japan's critics. His or her funding is not mentioned. Instead, he or she is identified only as an "eminent professor of Japanese studies at Big-Name U."[17]

Demonstrating that academic reality and parody are nearly indistinguishable, Packard in fact published such an op-ed piece in the *Washington Post*. This article, "The Japan Bashers Are Poisoning Foreign Policy," attacked critics of Japan's trade practices.[18] Packard was identified in the op-ed byline as "Dean of the Paul H. Nitze School of the Johns Hopkins University and director of its Center for East Asian Studies," rather than as a consultant. Packard also penned another op-ed article that appeared in the *New York Times*, contending that professors who had accepted Japanese funding were "patriotic" and had not "sold out to Japan," but never mentioning that he had received Japanese funding. The byline did not mention his consulting work.[19]

As is the case with newspapers, few social science journals require professorial authors to disclose their consulting work, expert testimony, or stock ownership, as leading medical journals now do; and few professors voluntarily divulge their corporate ties. For example, the American Psychological Association (APA), which publishes several highly respected academic journals and is one of the most influential social science associations to which professors belong, did not explicitly require its members to divulge conflicts of interest in published research articles until 1994. The APA's *Ethical Principles of Psychologists*, a manual setting forth the ethics expected of its members, is silent about "disclosing relationships (financial or otherwise) that present a possible conflict of interest," according to Leslie Cameron, who oversees the APA's publications.[20] The APA's *Publication Manual* suggested, but did not require, that authors use a footnote to "acknowledge...a grant or other financial support."[21] (The new edition of the *Manual*, released in mid-1994, requires disclosure. The disclosure statement was added after the APA received several queries about why it didn't have clear conflict-of-interest guidelines.)

Most academic organizations say even less about financial conflicts of interest than the APA.[22] Because these organizations do not require their members to disclose their consulting work, it is difficult to determine systematically how widespread consulting is among social science professors. However, the available systematic information suggests that consulting is very common, particularly in some disciplinary subfields (such as organizational communication, industrial psychology, and organizational sociology). A survey of members of the Speech Communication Association's Organizational Communication Division, for example, found that nearly three-quarters of the members worked as part-time consultants, although the majority of these made relatively little money from it.[23]

Taken for Granted

As noted in previous chapters, a professor's research and grant-getting record, not his or her teaching, are often the most important determinants of whether she or he is promoted and tenured. Successful grant fetchers are guaranteed tenure and can easily move to more prestigious institutions. According to university administrators, grants enhance the university's reputation and bring money into the university. However, although grants do bring in money, the real costs of conducting the research usually far exceed the amount of the grant.

Typical of corporate grants is one given by Union National Bank to two psychology professors at Western Michigan University in Kalamazoo, who conducted a study of piecework pay and worker productivity in the banking industry.[24] In another example, ABC Television provided two grants to University of Wisconsin at Madison researchers for studying "responses to television programming." The $40,000 was given by ABC to determine whether positive and negative emotional scenes are processed in different hemispheres of the brain. The grant produced several academic publications for the researchers with titles such as "Watching Television: Experiments on the Viewing Process" and "Emotional Television Scenes and Hemispheric Specialization."[25]

Corporate media like ABC and media groups are, in fact, frequent sources of grants. For example, the National Association of Broadcasters (NAB), the trade association of broadcasting corporations, also has a grants program for academics that consistently funds research beneficial to its members. In 1993, it funded five projects: "Meanings of Radio to its Potential Audience," at the University of Alabama; "Going Live: Is It Worth The Cost?," at Bethany College in Bethany, West Virginia; "Channel Loyalty: An Examination of Audience Behavior from the Perspectives of Broadcasters and Local Viewers," at Texas Christian University in Fort Worth; "Impact of Digital Cable Radio of In-Home Radio and Music Listening Habits," at Virginia Commonwealth University in Richmond; and "TV Station Experience and Satisfaction with Research Services," at California State University at San Bernadino. These research projects dealt with such "socially important" issues as whether live or taped news segments most impress news viewers, and whether television stations are happy with the Nielsen ratings service.

The academic research projects funded by the NAB in 1994 were equally self-serving. They had such titles as "Digital Radio Broadcasting Technology Applications," "Defining Patterns of TV Viewing," and "Accelerating the Flow: News Strategies for Prime-Time Program Transitions." This last project sought to determine how broadcasters could best hold onto their audiences. The NAB didn't fund any research on the relationship between commercials for running shoes and robbery, television's depictions of sex and rape, or the viewing of violent television programs and assaultive behavior—all of which are far more important social issues than television stations' satisfaction with their research services.

As is the case with professors in the other disciplines we have looked at, most social science professors who conduct research studies such as these are given reduced teaching responsibilities so they can pursue these "scholarly" projects. This reduction has increased class sizes, reduced professors' willingness to teach, and increased the number of classes taught by graduate students. And while the corporate grant may cover the direct costs of the research, students and taxpayers pay the salaries of the professors working on the corporate grant projects.[26]

Moreover, research funded by corporations and trade associations such as the NAB eventually gets published in scholarly journals. These publications tend to give such questionable research an air of respectability and help to justify the professors' light teaching loads. The articles get published because many journal editors simply assume that the research is important, since corporations, trade associations, or foundations have funded it. As a result, NAB-funded research reports on socially trivial topics such as "An Expanded, Integrated Model for Determining Audience Exposure to Television" and "Differences in the Consumption of Traditional Broadcast and VCR Movie Rentals" have found their way into print. The first article found that "a program's lead-in and lead-out" had the greatest effect on ratings; the second study found that people watch movie tapes more intently than television programs.[27]

The result is that social science research journals are increasingly filled with socially trivial articles, such as "Comparing Two Putting Styles for Putting Accuracy" (in *Perceptual & Motor Skills*[28]), "Social Networks and Tourist Behavior" (in *American Behavioral Scientist*[29]), "Communicative Effects of Gaze Behavior" (in *Human Communication Research*[30]), "What Audience Data Do Newspapers Provide Advertisers?" (in *Newspaper Research Journal*[31]), "Sources for Recipe Information" (in *Journalism Quarterly*[32]), "Is Narcissism Inversely Related to Satisfaction?" (in *Journal of Psychology*[33]), and "Does Specialization Affect Behavioral Choices and Quality Judgements Among Hunters?" (in *Leisure Sciences*).[34]

For such articles, many psychology, sociology, political science, and communications professors have been given reduced teaching responsibilities. As a congressional subcommittee report found, in the past faculty taught fifteen credits per semester and were also expected to engage in scholarship, serve on committees, advise students, develop curricula, and perform other tasks. Over time, the teaching load was reduced to twelve credits, then to nine, and at many places it is now six credits or lower.[35]

In 1994, the average teaching load for University of Wisconsin-Madison psychology faculty, for example, was three classes per academic year, or 3.75 hours per week of classroom lecturing. Some departments required slightly more teaching from their members. The linguistics faculty taught an average of two classes per semester or four classes per year, as did faculty in the department of library and information sciences.[36] Overall, faculty at the university spent 4.1 hours per week in classrooms teaching students.[37]

Although the public pays for much of the social science research—through reduced teaching responsibilities, grants given to faculty at state universities, and in numerous other ways—few members of the public ever hear about the research that's being conducted. One reason for this is that professors don't try to share their findings with the general public. A recent study examined the frequency with which academic researchers communicate with the public. The study examined the number of magazine articles written by the 53 most often published academic researchers in mass-communication studies, who collectively published 292 articles in academic journals between 1980 and 1985. During a ten-year period, the 53 professors managed to write a total of three magazine articles, which were liberally defined to include book reviews, op-ed articles, and almost anything else.[38]

Besides the two main sources of business influence discussed above—consulting fees and research grants from corporations and their foundations—corporations have been able to influence the social sciences in two other, more subtle ways. First, corporations and their foundations provide funding for specific programs of study that interest the corporation. For example, the Bell-South Foundation helped fund an interdisciplinary graduate program in telecommunication and education at the Georgia Institute of Technology in

Atlanta, and the Ameritech Foundation gave money to Michigan State University's College of Communication, which teaches a few courses in telephony and new telecommunication technologies. In times of university budget cuts and downsizing, programs like these that have received outside funding are likely to go unscathed; programs that haven't, on the other hand, are likely to be reduced in size or even eliminated.

A second, but far more significant, influence is that corporations and their foundations have become sacred cows to university administrators. Few professors are willing to jeopardize their standing in universities by publishing research articles critical of these donors. For example, a professor at a university receiving Ameritech funding who dared to conduct research on the detrimental effects of Ameritech lobbying would be ostracized—or even terminated, if untenured. This worshipful attitude toward corporate funding helps explain why social science research, while often trivial, is rarely critical of corporate practices.

Chapter Six

The Centers for Corporate Research

On a summer-like day in mid-September 1993, members of College Republicans at the University of Wisconsin at Milwaukee (UWM) unfurled a banner reading "UWM College Republicans Love Tommy." The banner referred to Republican governor "Tommy" Thompson, who was to address a ceremony that morning commemorating the opening of UWM's $11 million architecture building.

Governor Thompson was joined at the podium by James Keyes, the chief executive officer of Johnson Controls, Inc., a manufacturer of electrical controls for heating, ventilation, and air conditioning systems, and the nation's largest supplier of plastic bottles and containers.[1] Keyes was there to announce that Johnson Controls was providing a $1 million, five-year grant to UWM for the Johnson Controls Institute, a research center that would study "environmental control" within buildings. The new corporate-funded institute would be housed in the $11 million, taxpayer-funded architecture building.

At the ceremony, speakers talked about the environment, ecological damage, and Johnson Controls' interests in maintaining a healthy environment. "The Johnson Controls Institute for Environmental Quality in Architecture will ultimately help industry create a more productive building," Keyes said. "It is hoped that the institute will become a worldwide mecca for ideas from both the academic world and industry on how to make buildings and the people who work in them more productive." No speaker mentioned that Johnson Controls is the nation's leading manufacturer of plastic containers, which are a major source of pollution and environmental damage.

Keyes wasn't the only Johnson Controls executive in attendance that morning. The audience was filled with Johnson Controls public relations flaks, who struck up conversations with reporters to say that "workers and students can be more productive when a building's heating, cooling, lighting and sound systems are properly controlled." The institute would determine the factors within buildings that make workers more productive, these Johnson Controls employees said.

The institute, which the company hopes will be a boon to its buildings controls division, will be run by "a committee of representatives from UWM and Johnson Controls and others, [who] would decide which of several proposed research projects would receive grant money," said the press release announcing the institute's creation.[2]

Over the next five years, Johnson Controls, Inc. will contribute $200,000 annually to the institute. For their $200,000, Johnson Controls is getting access to research for far less than the actual cost. The ten UWM professors and two graduate students who comprise the institute's staff earn just under $500,000 a year in total salaries (not counting benefits), which are paid by Wisconsin taxpayers. Since the research produced by the institute will bear the University of Wisconsin affiliation, it will be more credible than in-house research.

The new UWM institute is typical of numerous business-funded institutes that have been created on college campuses. These institutes conduct research of interest to a company or industry and answer to business through a representative that sits on the institute's board of directors.

One of the first institutes of this type—slavishly devoted to industry—was established at New York University in 1972. The money for the Salomon Brothers Center for the Study of Financial Institutions, which is now referred to as the New York University Salomon Center, was provided by the brokerage firm Salomon Brothers, Inc. to "underwrite applied academic research, conduct conferences for scholars and practitioners, engage in specialized executive education," and publish journals for the financial services industry.[3] The money was given to NYU to create "an important link between scholars, practioners and regulators concerned with financial institutions"; it was not given to improve undergraduate education or assist NYU students.

Like the Johnston Controls Institute, the Salomon Center has an advisory board drawn from industry. The board's chair is Martin Leibowitz, managing director of Salomon Brothers. Other members are from Chemical Bank, Merrill Lynch, Standard & Poor's, and J.P. Morgan and Co. With advice and financial assistance from these corporations, the Salomon Center has been able to hold conferences, conduct research, and even produce publications (such as *The Journal of Derivatives*, published jointly by the Center and *Institutional Investor*, a trade publication for the financial services industry) that are designed to assist the investment industry.[4]

In 1975, a similar institute devoted to oil and gas, one of Texas's major industries, was established at Southern Methodist University (SMU) in Dallas. There, Cary M. Maguire, the chairman, president, and chief executive officer of Maguire Oil Co., who also served as a member of SMU's board of trustees and board of governors, established the Maguire Oil and Gas Institute.[5] According to SMU, the purpose of the Maguire Oil and Gas Institute "is to advance productive working relations with key industrial and government leaders, and with academic departments and programs that complement the Institute's work. The Institute is developing national academic programs and publications related to the changing environment of the oil and gas industry."[6]

In practice, this meant hiring John A. Baden, a hard-right anti-environmentalist, as the institute's director. Before being named director of the Maguire Oil and Gas Institute, Baden had established solid, anti-environmentalist credentials, having founded a right-wing think tank in Bozeman, Montana that criticized environmental laws. He also served as an "adjunct scholar" with the Cato Institute, a Washington-based, conservative think tank (see Chapter Seven). In publications such as *Policy Review*, the magazine of the conservative Heritage Foundation, Baden berated government regulators, rather than industrialists like Maguire, for causing environmental damage.

While at the SMU institute, he penned such articles as "Crimes Against Nature: Public Funding Of Environmental Destruction" and "Oil and Environmentalism Do Mix."[7] His articles contended that

> Instead of harmonizing oil and gas discoveries with environ-
> mental goals, [environmental laws] have resulted in an extrava-
> gant amount of federal land being placed off-limits to oil and gas
> leasing. And those lands still "open" to leasing suffer severe,
> costly and ill-conceived restrictions...Many scientific studies and
> a wealth of anecdotal evidence attest that oil and gas operations
> can be conducted without harm to sensitive areas...Experience in
> Alaska, Michigan and Wyoming show that oil and gas activity,
> with proper care and supervision, can be compatible with the en-
> vironment.[8]

The Howdy Doody Centers

Since the founding of the Salomon Center and Maguire Institute, numerous corporate-sponsored institutes have been established on college campuses. In contrast to the Johnson Controls
Institute, Salomon Center, and the Maguire Oil and Gas Institute,
which are principally funded by one corporation, some "research"
centers are funded by entire industries. For example, the Garn Institute of Finance at the University of Utah is funded by a host of
banks, savings and loans, and other lenders. Still other centers, financed by foreign governments or foreign corporations, serve as
supportive spokespersons for foreign policies beneficial to their
benefactors. Many of these university-based research centers are
more lobbyist than laboratory, more puppet than pedagogue.

One of the most Howdy Doody-like of the corporate research
centers is the Garn Institute of Finance, established at the University of Utah in 1986, two years before the savings and loan scandal
became public. The institute is named after ex-senator Jake Garn,
who co-sponsored the S&L bill that deregulated the industry and
produced widespread fraud and losses. The Garn bill allowed savings and loans to move into speculative investments like junk
bonds. The bill also allowed owners of S&Ls to lend money to themselves, opening the vault doors to people like Lincoln Savings' Charles Keating and Midwest Savings' Hal Greenwood—both notorious
S&L operators now serving prison terms.

Although the Garn Institute claims that it exists to conduct
"financial services research and study," it is more accurately de-

scribed as a pseudonymous trade group of the financial services industry. It has taken meetings between people like Charles Keating and the Keating Five out of smoke-filled rooms and moved them into university classrooms. It also provides a setting where bankers can publicly lobby federal regulators and legislators.

A listing of the institute's founders and officers is a virtual litany of abuse within the S&L industry. To repay Senator Garn for deregulating the S&L industry, some of the most reckless savings and loans in the country provided seed money for the institute. Founding members, who gave $100,000 or more to the institute, include the now-bankrupt Columbia Savings and Loan of Beverly Hills, Centrust Savings Bank of Miami, and Imperial Corp. of San Diego. (These bankruptcies cost U.S. taxpayers about $6 billion.) Great Western Bank of Beverly Hills, which took over several bankrupt savings and loans at fire-sale prices, was also a founding member, as was defunct junk-bond dealer Drexel Burnham Lambert.

The chairman of the Garn Institute's board of directors is Richard T. Pratt, chairman of Merrill Lynch Mortgage Capital. Dick Pratt was President Reagan's first chairman of the Federal Home Loan Bank Board, which oversaw S&Ls. In *The Greatest-Ever Bank Robbery*, economic analyst Martin Mayer wrote that Pratt "had fired the guards and suspended the rules...if you had to pick one individual to blame for what happened to the S&Ls and to some hundreds of billions of dollars in taxpayer money, Dick would get the honor without even campaigning."

Elaine Weis, a former Utah State Department of Financial Institutions commissioner, is also a director of the Garn Institute. A blue-ribbon panel investigating the collapse of Utah's deposit insurance system reported that Weis, while commissioner, carried out a five-year disinformation campaign to hide the insolvency of the industry. The panel concluded that Weis headed a complex scheme to mislead citizens about the health of S&Ls and the state's insurance fund. A memo that she wrote reported, "I think we've been pretty successful in putting out a good story as to why depositors shouldn't be concerned. I don't know why anybody believes it." The subsequent investigation concluded that her "conduct, if done by any private citizen, would not only constitute fraud, it would be a felony."[9]

What exactly does the Garn Institute do? For one thing, the center spends about $90,000 annually on various events, including an annual Downhill Conference at a Utah ski resort, according to its financial report. (Money for this and other institute activities comes from two dozen banks, credit companies, and trade associations, such as National Association of Homebuilders and the Consumer Bankers Association.) Typical of these events is the "scholarly conference" held on February 7-9, 1991 at the university. Of twenty-eight speakers at the conference, only three were professors. The other participants were government regulators, legislators, bankers, and lobbyists, who schmoozed together and talked about policies that might be adopted or changed.

Sears and Roebuck's senior vice president David Shute typified the "scholarship" exhibited at this conference. He pressed for passage of House Bill H.R. 192, which would allow Sears to get into the banking business. Shute declared, "We at Sears believe significant, substantive changes to the structure and operations of the U.S. financial services industry are absolutely necessary to maintain, and more important, enhance the competitiveness of U.S. financial services institutions. We also believe many of those changes can be effected through the passage of legislation pending in Congress called the 'Depository Institution Affiliation Act,' or H.R. 192. Sears strongly supports this legislation."[10]

As is clear from this example, these centers are essentially hubs of corporate influence. A few on-campus research centers, such as the Iacocca Institute for Economic Competitiveness at Lehigh University in Bethlehem, Pennsylvania, even admit openly that their primary goal is to serve industry rather than students. The Iacocca Institute was established at former Chrysler CEO Lee Iacocca's alma mater with his assistance in 1987. Iacocca pledged $1 million of his own money and another $1.5 million from Chrysler to help Lehigh purchase a mountaintop research park from Bethlehem Steel to serve as the institute's home.[11] To help raise the $40 million needed to purchase the research park, Chrysler put the squeeze on its 5,000 dealers, asking each to donate $1,000 to Lehigh. The "donations," Chrysler said, could be charged against the dealers' parts accounts.[12] Fund-raising techniques of this sort were successful, and Lehigh University raised enough money to purchase and rehabilitate the research park, which opened with hoopla in June 1991.

The Iacocca Institute established an advisory board consisting almost exclusively of corporate executives, including Iacocca, Bethlehem Steel CEO Walter F. Williams, Union Pacific CEO Drew Lewis, and USX CEO David Roderick. The only "academicians" on the advisory board were Lehigh University president Peter Likins and former United Auto Workers boss Douglas Fraser, whom institute literature touted as the "university professor of labor studies at Wayne State University." At its first meeting, the advisory board decided that the "Institute, rather than being just a think-tank, would act as a catalyst to begin action-oriented programs to strengthen U.S. manufacturing," which at the time was being pummeled and degraded by Japanese manufacturers.[13]

The first conference held by the institute attracted 150 industry executives, not professors, who brainstormed about how "U.S. manufacturers [could] develop a vision for future development of manufacturing technologies to serve both Department of Defense and U.S. manufacturing needs."[14] The conference led to the creation of the Agile Manufacturing Enterprise Forum, a division within the Iacocca Institute. According to the Iacocca Institute, the forum "is an industry-led group which includes more than 100 individual companies, professional organizations, consortia, and government agencies," not an educational enterprise.[15] Its purpose is to promote "agile manufacturing" technology, which will allow U.S. corporations to rapidly change manufacturing processes to adjust to changes in the marketplace.

Franc Scholarship

In addition to corporations and industries, foreign countries have realized that a little money goes a long way in buying influence at universities. Giving money to a university to establish a "center" is tax-deductible, cheaper than hiring lobbyists, and can help a country achieve its foreign-policy goals, just as funding a university center can help a corporation or industry achieve its goals.

On February 23, 1994, the *New York Times* noted that "fearful of losing political and cultural status, France is giving money to six major American universities in the hope of creating a new generation of Francophiles."[16] The article referred to a 1994 grant of $400,000 that France had given to six universities—Harvard, Princeton, Johns Hopkins, Berkeley, the University of Chicago, and the University of Pennsylvania—that would be used to create six "Centers of Excellence in French Studies." Earlier, Germany had created centers for German studies at Georgetown, Harvard, and Berkeley.

As another example, at the University of Minnesota a member of Taiwan's Kuomingtang central committee and owner of Taiwan's largest circulation, pro-government newspaper funds the *China Times* Center for Media and Social Studies. The center's purpose is "to promote China's democracy,"[17] which it does by promoting Taiwan's anti-China campaign.

At the center's first conference in October 1989, repression in China, which was technically at war with Taiwan, was the topic of most presentations. These presentations were made by a handful of Chinese defectors and a number of professors and journalists, several of whom were from Taiwan and Hong Kong.[18] Taiwanese repression, including the much-publicized arrest and prosecution of Taiwan dissident Hsu Hsin-liang, never made it onto the conference agenda.

In another example of the influence of foreign countries, Saudi Arabia has been bankrolling an Islamic Law Center at Harvard Law School since 1993. The $5 million in Saudi funds for the Islamic Law Center was described by Saudi Prince Bandar bin Sultan as "part of the King's efforts to serve Islam worldwide." Professor Frank Vogel of Harvard Law School described the money as a gift without restrictions.[19]

Another example of the ties between foreign countries and university institutes is Johns Hopkins. Johns Hopkins's Center for East Asian Studies, which Dean George Packard directs, gets about 10 percent of its annual budget from Japanese government agencies and corporations, including Nomura Securities, Toyota, and NEC.[20] Johns Hopkins's Center for Talented Youth has received funding from the Toyota Foundation, and Johns Hopkins's National Foreign Language Center has received funding from the U.S.-Japan Foundation. The U.S.-Japan Foundation was founded by Ryoichi Sasakawa, a Japanese nationalist who was jailed for war crimes by the

Allies after World War II. Sasakawa's postwar fortune was made principally from gambling.[21]

Many other universities have also received large sums of money from Sasakawa. In 1993, the U.S.-Japan Foundation gave $100,000 or more to the University of Maryland, Columbia University, the University of Kansas, Mississippi State University in State College, Mississippi, Indiana University, and East Carolina University in Greensville, North Carolina.[22] Dozens of other universities—including Harvard, Princeton University in Princeton, New Jersey, Tufts, Yale, and York University in Toronto, Canada—have taken money from Sasakawa or one of his "philanthropic foundations." Duke University received more than $1 million from Sasakawa to start the Asia/Pacific Studies Institute.

In fact, one of the few universities that has *not* accepted money from Sasakawa is the University of Hawaii, which is a stone's throw from Pearl Harbor. The director of the University of Hawaii's Center for Japanese Studies, Patricia Steinhoff, told the *Chronicle of Higher Education* that her institution would not accept a grant from Sasakawa because of his background "and the sources of his funds." Professor Steinhoff said that "there was more to be lost by accepting [Sasakawa's] money."[23]

A similar view is expressed by Professor Bob Wakabayashi, who resigned as director of York University's East Asian Studies Program after his university accepted money from Sasakawa. Wakabayashi believes that Sasakawa is "working hand in glove with the Japanese government to white-wash their war record."[24]

Others, such as authors John Judis and Pat Choate, see such donations as doing much more than just whitewashing war records. The donations of Sasakawa and others have made U.S. scholars who study Japan extremely dependent on the Japanese for research funding, travel money, and scholarships. Nearly 80 percent of funding for American research about Japan comes from Japan, and this undoubtedly effects the content of research—because professors supportive of Japanese policy goals get funded, but professors critical of Japan do not.[25] Moreover, because Japanese-funded professors are able to conduct what appears to be "higher quality" research—involving travel to Japan, meetings with high-level Japanese leaders, and access to Japanese corporations—their research generates far more publicity than research of other professors. This publicity influences the views that scholars and citizens develop about Japan.

Other Research Centers

Centers created by university administrators and departments—rather than corporations, tycoons, or foundations—far outnumber the centers funded by special interest groups. However, these centers also pander to corporate interests in order to receive funding. They provide consultants to businesses, conduct research for companies, dole out advice to entrepreneurs, or perform any other act—for a small fee. The growth of these centers is chronicled in the *Research Centers Directory*, a publication listing on- and off-campus research organizations in a variety of science, social science, and business fields. In 1982, 5,422 research centers were listed in the *Directory*. By 1993, over 13,000 research centers were listed. University-related research offices and parks had 210 entries in 1982 and 421 in 1993.[26]

Almost all of the university-based research centers of this type are funded by a combination of university and industry funds. But the majority of dollars appears to come from the universities themselves, either directly or indirectly in the form of reduced teaching responsibilities for professors, tuition waivers for research assistants, and the like. In effect, these on-campus research centers provide corporations with indirect research-and-development subsidies.

For example, Georgia State University's Center for Mature Consumer Studies researches the "purchasing habits and consumption patterns" of older Americans. The center describes itself as though it were a marketing-research agency rather than an educational enterprise, doing "syndicated studies, research consulting, customized market reports and customized analyses" for sponsors.[27] The center's literature explains that "companies [can] suggest topics, and custom studies are conducted on a per request basis."

The center's director, who describes himself as having "consulted with businesses such as BellSouth, Coca-Cola, Black & Decker, Chase Manhattan and American Express on the consumer behavior of older adults," is the author of *Marketing to Older Con-*

sumers: A Handbook for Information Strategy Development. This is a book "to help practitioners better understand older consumers in order to more effectively design and market products and services to this segment of the population." He has also published such "scholarly" articles as "Use of Credit Cards by Older Americans."[28] For this work, the center's director gets an annual salary of $94,545, reduced teaching responsibilities, and assignments to teach small graduate courses, rather than large undergraduate courses.[29]

There are several other similar centers at Georgia State—such as the Center for Risk Management and Insurance Research and the Economic Forecasting Center—which also list their "parent institution" (a code word for taxpayers and students) as the first source of funding. As with the Center for Mature Consumer Studies, the Economic Forecasting Center solicits companies to sponsor it. The annual sponsorship fee is $4,000; associate sponsorship is available for $2,000.[30]

Almost all universities, with the exception of small liberal-arts colleges, have similar research centers. Bowling Green State University in Bowling Green, Ohio has the Management Center, which "conducts research, consulting, and management development programs, including projects in strategic planning, market research... and international business" for companies. Bradley University's Center for Business and Economic Research in Peoria, Illinois provides companies with "program evaluation, economic development, market research, impact analysis, modeling, forecasting, survey research, cost and price modeling." Iowa State University in Ames, Iowa operates the Center for Industrial Research and Service, which provides assistance in "manufacturing, technology transfer, productivity, new product design, manufacturing processes, marketing and related topics;" and the Midwest Agribusiness Trade Research and Information Center, which seeks to "expand international trade in agribusiness products" by conducting "market studies [that] focus on product markets and geographical markets." These centers, like others, are dependent on the parent institution for funds, and this dependency means that tax and tuition dollars are providing subsidies to businesses.

Even more expensive to construct and administer have been "research parks," which are multi-acre complexes built and operated by universities where space is leased to new and established corporations. The parks include research laboratories, incubator space, and sometimes manufacturing centers and warehouses. The parks are typically joint efforts between a university and a private developer, both hoping to lure corporations to set up shop on their grounds with promises of cheap leases and access to professorial expertise. Their construction is supported by state legislators, who hope that the research parks will attract businesses and jobs to the region. Universities support the construction of research parks because, like other projects, the parks have the potential of bringing corporate dollars onto the campus. But like most other university-business endeavors, the parks have had the opposite impact—syphoning money away from education.

The number of research parks has grown immensely during the last decade and a half, as has their cost.[31] The costs of constructing the parks are high because they are usually built on undeveloped land and require investments in roads and highways, landscaping, sewer and water services, natural gas, security services, and the like. These expenses are above and beyond the costs of the land, and the tax breaks and subsidies that the parks get from local governments, all of which divert tax dollars from educational and social programs to businesses.

An example of these parks is the Connecticut Technology Park. The University of Connecticut started the Connecticut Technology Park in 1983, promising that it would attract businesses and jobs and would be cost-free to taxpayers. The park was to include a hotel, conference center, apartments, and one million square feet of industrial building space, located on 390 acres of university land.[32]

As of 1993, however, none of the promises had been fulfilled. As a result of squabbles between the university and its partners in the venture, the state wound up allocating $2.7 million for building some roads for the park, and pledging $4.2 million more to complete the project.[33] The state also gave the university's park corporation another half-million dollars for salaries and other expenses; and the federal government came up with money for the park as part of a $17.4 million pork-barrel grant to advance research at the university and spur economic development in the region.[34] Despite these massive subsidies, the park has yet to attract any tenants.

Even when such parks are located on campuses, they can still cost a lot of money. The University of Delaware spent about $1.5 million in university, state, and federal funds to construct a research park at its campus on the Delaware Bay, hoping that its marine sciences center would be a magnet to industry. "In eight years, the park has had no takers," the *Chronicle of Higher Education* reports.[35]

The university research parks that have been successful have promised their corporate tenants that they would provide these tenants with easy, and inexpensive, access to professorial expertise. For example, the Central Florida Research Park, which was established by the University of Central Florida and Orange County, creates "an environment which promotes and fosters relationships between industry and the university." The Iowa State University Research Park facilitates "interaction between corporate research laboratories and the University research community." And the University of Iowa's Oakdale Research Park promises tenants that it "provides opportunities for businesses to work with University faculty."[36]

These parks have not only drained resources from communities and universities, but they have also failed to achieve their major goal of increasing regional employment. A study found that just 16 of 45 university research parks were successful in increasing regional employment, whereas 19 were unsuccessful. The remainder had no impact on employment at all.[37] Overall, the major beneficiaries of the parks have been a few high-tech businesses that set up shop in the parks to get cheap rent and access to professorial expertise.

Chapter Seven

Right-Thinking Campus Think Tanks

In *Impostors in the Temple*, former Reagan administration economic adviser Martin Anderson charges that at universities today, "teaching is low man on the totem pole of academic prestige. What counts today is research and publishing and certain kinds of administrative work. Professors get prestigious positions, promotions, and salary increases primarily on the work they do as researchers and administrators, not teachers...And many of them have sloughed off their teaching responsibilities with skill and dispatch."[1]

Similarly, in the *Washington Post*, Anderson published an op-ed article titled, "The Gall of Ivy: Our Professors Do Everything But Teach," which asserted that universities were corrupted by "the well-publicized menace of 'political correctness'" and professors' refusals to teach. Anderson compared professors' teaching responsibilities with a "Ponzi scheme or real estate fraud," where students and their parents are duped into paying for an education that they do not get.[2]

Although he criticizes universities and professors for promoting research instead of teaching, Anderson himself is a university-based "researcher" who never enters the classroom. He works at Stanford University's Hoover Institution, an on-campus think tank specializing in right-wing policy reports, not teaching. Rather than teaching, Anderson spends his time criticizing professors and promoting economic policies, such as cutting the capital gains tax rate, that benefit corporate moguls.[3]

Although Anderson is outspokenly critical of universities for squandering students' money on non-educational programs, he is silent about the Hoover Institution's plundering of Stanford dollars for non-educational programs. During the 1990-91 academic year, over $4 million from Stanford University's general funds were poured into the Hoover Institution—at the expense of educational programs.[4]

The Hoover Institution is the largest and best-known on-campus conservative think tank, but it's not the only one. Many universities house similar centers of right-think. And like Anderson, many of the loudest critics of universities, who assert that professors promote political correctness and shirk their teaching responsibilities, are associated with these on-campus think tanks, which operate at the expense of education. For example, the late Allan Bloom—author of *The Closing of the American Mind*, which claimed that 1960s activists "were the source of the collapse of the entire American educational structure"[5]—was co-director of the John M. Olin Center for Inquiry into the Theory and Practice of Democracy at the University of Chicago. Because of his administrative and research responsibilities at the center, Bloom had reduced teaching responsibilities.[6]

Although they criticize left-leaning professors' teaching, these conservative critics are not the role models that they pretend to be. Rather than preparing and delivering lectures, they work at on-campus think tanks that produce and distribute right-wing and pro-corporate propaganda tracts disguised as research, while simultaneously denouncing the politicization of college campuses. The policies advocated by these centers, such as decreased government intervention in the economy, invariably benefit their corporate patrons rather than the public. For example, the Center for the Study of Public Choice, a think tank at George Mason University, claims that "our politicians hail the demise of socialism in far away places, as they proceed to blunt incentives in this country with higher taxes, more regulations, larger deficits, job quotas, more transfer programs, Clean Air Acts and a host of other politicized interventions. It seems clear now that Ronald Reagan was not enough, and, indeed, that he did not seize the day in the early 1980's to make the kind of radical changes in the structure of our political economy that would have reversed the century-long drift toward collectivization-politicization." The center advocates eliminating regulations that govern most business practices.[7]

The Hoover Institution: The First Among Many

The Hoover Institution on War, Revolution and Peace at Stanford University began as the Hoover War Library in 1919. Herbert Hoover, a Stanford alumnus, donated $50,000 to Stanford for assembling and preserving documents about World War I, the League of Nations, and the Bolshevik revolution.

During its first decades of operation, the Hoover Institution was content to acquire documents, produce bibliographies, and publish anthologies of documents from the World War I era. Its role changed during the anti-communist hysteria of the 1950s, when the library's patron, Herbert Hoover, declared that his namesake needed to produce books and other materials to "demonstrate the evils of the doctrines of Karl Marx...and to reaffirm the validity of the American system."[8]

The library became an independent institution on the Stanford campus in 1959, operating outside the normal university governance procedures. Hoover "scholars" enjoyed the prestige associated with being at Stanford but were neither required to teach nor to produce traditional scholarship.

The reconstituted Hoover Institution answered to Stanford's board of trustees, not to the faculty, and was to conduct and publish anti-communist "research." W. Glenn Campbell, a conservative who had worked for six years at the American Enterprise Institute, a Washington think tank and champion of corporate capitalism, was brought in to head the Hoover Institution. He was personally selected for the post by President Hoover.

From 1960 to 1990, the size and influence of the Hoover Institution grew. It went from six "fellows" in 1960 to 85 in 1990, and had another 71 "visiting scholars" in residence that year. During 1990, it had an administrative staff of 31, and an additional 36 research assistants and support staffers. Its endowment exceeded $125 million, and its annual operating budget was over $15 million.[9]

The money for the institution comes from Stanford, corporations, conservative tycoons, and right-wing foundations, all of which have close ties to the Hoover Institution through its board of overseers. Its board includes rightist tycoons like brewer Joseph Coors and financier Shelby Cullom Davis, who donate large sums to numerous conservative causes. Also on the board are publishing magnates such as Rupert Murdoch of News America Corp., oil company executives such as Charles Sitter of Exxon Corp., and heads of conservative foundations such as William Simon, a former Nixon administration official and president of the John M. Olin Foundation.[10]

The Hoover Institution's affluence and size are just two of the reasons why it is the most important of the on-campus conservative "thinks." Another is that its fellows are interconnected with many right-wing think tanks and foundations, and these relations provide them with influence within a national network of conservative institutions. Hoover fellows are directors or advisers to such off-campus think tanks as the Heritage Foundation and American Enterprise Institute, and such conservative foundations as Smith Richardson and Earhart, which provide think tanks with funding[11] (see sidebar on off-campus think tanks).

Other Think Tanks

Other think tanks have mimicked Hoover's structure, with boards of advisers, funding from right-wing foundations and corporations, and institutional agreements that keep the think tanks outside of normal university governance procedures. These structures insulate them from faculty scrutiny and funding cuts. For example, the Center for International Security and Strategic Studies at Mississippi State University has an advisory board that includes a retired U.S. Marine Corps general, a Hughes Aircraft Corporation executive, a representative of the U.S. Secretary of Defense, and the university's president. Its underwriters include oil companies, banks, right-wing foundations, and the U.S.-Japan Foundation.[12]

Universities welcome these think tanks because they bring substantial amounts of money to the university and create an ideological climate in which university-corporate ties can easily flourish. For example, the Social Philosophy and Policy Center at Bowling Green State University took in three times as much foundation money in 1989-90 as all other units at the university combined. It also produced a spate of articles criticizing employment, antidiscrimination, comparable worth, and sexual harassment laws that govern business practices. Concerning sexual harassment laws, Ellen Frankel Paul, the center's deputy director, wrote that the most "distressing" part of

The Off-Campus Think Tanks

Dozens of off-campus conservative think tanks operate in the United States. Most are closely associated with on-campus think tanks. The American Enterprise Institute (AEI), Heritage Foundation, National Forum Foundation, Capital Research Center, Center for Strategic and International Studies (CSIS), Competitive Enterprise Institute, Cato Institute, and Free Congress Foundation are based in or around Washington, D.C. Beyond the beltway are the Manhattan Institute (New York), Urban Policy Research Institute (Ohio), James Madison Institute (Florida), Yankee Center for Public Policy Studies (Connecticut), John Locke Foundation (North Carolina), Institute for Contemporary Studies (California), Goldwater Institute (Arizona), Rockford Institute (Illinois), Heartland Institute (Illinois), and Political Economy Research Center (Montana), to name but a handful.

There are dozens of rightist think tanks, but only a few left-leaning think tanks. All think tanks claim to be nonpartisan, which merely means that they do not formally endorse or campaign for candidates running for public office. Because they are legally nonpartisan, they are eligible for nonprofit, tax exempt status, so that businesses and corporate mandarins get tax writeoffs for their contributions to them.

Although legally nonpartisan, the think tanks are more appropriately described as "advocacy centers," reports *Time* magazine.[13] The think tanks churn out policy papers, reports and press releases supporting conservative policy proposals. The think tanks have also been very successful at getting media attention, something that university administrators also seek for their institutions. Studies by Fairness and Accuracy in Reporting (FAIR), a left-leaning media watchdog group, found that these think tanks provide numerous experts for news shows such as the "MacNeil/Lehrer NewsHour."[14]

The problem isn't that their research is highly partisan—one would expect it to be—it's that they try to pass off shopworn rhetoric as research. The difference between old-time conservative rhetoric and think-tank output is that the former was presented at American Legion halls on Friday nights over beer, while the latter is sandwiched between well-designed covers and called "research." This criticism of think tank research isn't expressed just by members of the political left; it is voiced by everyone who conducts legitimate research.

Some think-tank leaders are more open about their partisanship than others. Former Heritage Foundation vice president Burton Pines described the foundation's purpose as "provid[ing] conservative policy-makers with arguments to bolster our side." Heritage spokesman Phillip Truluck said "[Our] goal is a conservative nation."[15] Other conservative think tanks, such as the American Enterprise Institute, are not as open about their purpose, despite a consensus on the Left and Right about where they lie on the political spectrum.[16]

The think tanks frequently use the term "scholar" to describe the individuals associated with them, thereby enhancing the status of the think tanks and their spokespersons. Former Reagan and Bush administration appointees are the "scholars" in residence at these think tanks. Linda Chavez, former staff director for the U.S. Civil Rights Commission, is with the Manhattan Institute; former U.S. Department of Education appointee Mitch Pearlstein heads the Center of the American Experiment; Richard T. Allen, T. Kenneth Cribb, and Ed Meese joined the Heritage Foundation after leaving government; former national security adviser Robert McFarlane and former State Department staffers Stephen Sestanovich and Leo Reddy went to the Center for Strategic and International Studies; and the American Enterprise Institute gave shelter to over two dozen high-level Reagan appointees.

The annual budget of any one of the big conservative thinks tanks exceeds the combined budgets of all left-of-center think tanks combined. The AEI had a $10 million budget in 1990; most of it came from corporations.[17] One-third of the CSIS's $9 million budget came from corporate coffers, as did $2.5 million of the Heritage Foundation's $14.6 million budget.[18] The largest share of Heritage's contributions came from conservative fat cats like Adolph Coors, Union Pacific chairman Drew Lewis, Amway chairman Jay Van Andel, and investment banker Shelby Cullom Davis.[19]

With so many resources available, the right-wing think tanks should be able to conduct very serious research, but they don't. In 1986, the late Timothy S. Healy, president of Georgetown University, initiated an academic review of the CSIS, which at the time was affiliated with, but not under the control of, the university. The review examined the scholarship of CSIS fellows, who, like most think-tank denizens, spent more time doing television soundbites than serious thinking. The CSIS attempted to derail the review by charging that it was politically motivated and, when this was shown to be false, arguing that the review was pointless because "the university is not a top-flight university."[20]

Healy appointed a committee of five highly respected academics from outside the university to review the CSIS's work. The committee concluded that center fellows produced partisan propaganda, not scholarship. After reviewing the committee's report, the trustees of Georgetown severed relations with the CSIS. The CSIS thereafter became an independent, off-campus think tank.[21]

The credentials of "scholars" at other off-campus think tanks aren't any stronger than those at the CSIS. To mask the academic anemia of their "scholars," conservative think tanks have created their own "research" journals. The journals bear names that closely resemble those of legitimate academic journals, and are used to inflate their spokespersons' credentials. The AEI created *Public Opinion*, a counterfeit version of *Public Opinion Quarterly*, a respected social-science journal that has been published since 1937. The Heritage Foundation publishes *Policy Review*, not the highly regarded *Policy Sciences*. The Institute for Contemporary Studies publishes the *Journal of Contemporary Studies*.

These publications pass for scholarly journals because some of their authors have university affiliations, often via on-campus think tanks. For example, Hoover Institution fellows wrote for publications of the Institute for Contemporary Studies, CSIS, Cato Institute, Heritage Foundation, and AEI, according to the Hoover Institution's *Report 1990*.

The think-tank journals are crammed with articles like "Bleak House: The Democrats' Doomsday Message," "The Straight Story on Homosexuality and Gay Rights," and "The Soundness of Our Structure: Confidence in the Reagan Years," which claim to be social science but read like the Republican National Platform.

Moreover, the articles in these journals, rather than legitimate academic journals, have produced the "impressive credentials" of many of their employees. For example, AEI resident scholar William Schneider published 16 articles in *Public*

Opinion during the 1980s, but not a single article in *Public Opinion Quarterly*.

Think tanks also utilize "adjunct scholars" to enhance their academic status. The adjunct scholars are usually professors associated with on-campus think tanks. For example, the Cato Institute's adjunct scholars include Thomas DiLorenzo of the University of Tennessee in Chatanooga's Center for Economic Education, Walter Grinder of George Mason University's Institute for Humane Studies, Henry Manne of George Mason University's Law and Economics Center, and Sam Peltzman of the University of Chicago's Center for the Study of the Economy and the State.[22]

While the research of most think-tank denizens isn't serious, their lobbying efforts on behalf of corporate contributors are. In addition to publishing endless tracts that promote capital gains tax cuts, deregulation, and unfettered corporate capitalism, the think tanks engage in some very donor-specific projects. For example, the Heritage Foundation, which received more than $3 million of its $18 million endowment from Taiwanese corporations, has been very active in promoting issues of concern to Taiwan's businesses. Heritage escorted congressional staff members to Taiwan, sponsored conferences on U.S.-Taiwan free trade to which it invited U.S. policymakers and the media, and promoted the idea of a "Free Trade Area Agreement" with Taiwan similar to that which the United States has with Canada and Mexico. It publishes pamphlets such as "U.S. Policy Toward China's Reunification" that promote Taiwan's positions.[23]

Two of the Taiwanese corporations that donate to the Heritage Foundation also give large sums to the American Enterprise Institute. Since receiving these donations, the AEI has sponsored conferences, seminars, and publications that promote Taiwanese positions. For example, the AEI sponsored two large conferences to which Washington officials were invited. One praised the emergence of democracy in the capitalist East, while the second examined security in Asia. The latter was held in Taiwan. The AEI also held four seminars about Taiwan issues, such as Taiwan-U.S. relations and the People's Republic of China's military buildup.[24]

Title VII of the Civil Rights Act of 1964 is that "the primary target of litigations is not the actual harasser, but rather the employer." The legislation unfairly targets businesses, Frankel Paul asserted.[25] Concerning antidiscrimation laws, she wrote:

> Antidiscrimination laws of various sorts, especially those like the Equal Pay Act of 1963, which commands equal pay for equal work, will operate to distort those natural market forces by preventing the disfavored from offering their services at lower rates, and thus will hurt their intended beneficiaries. Another effect of antidiscrimination laws is to limit the information that employers are permitted to gather about particular employees.[26]

Needless to say, the article favored changing laws so that corporations have freer reign in hiring, paying, and promoting employees.

Another think tank, the Institute of Humane Studies at George Mason University, raked in $1.54 million in 1990 and had assets of $2.69 million. This think tank received funding from the Olin, Scaife, and other right-wing foundations, and from such "socially responsible" corporations as R. J. Reynolds, Philip Morris, and Arco.[27] The institute is opposed to government regulation of the economy, instead favoring "volunteerism in all human relations," "protection of those rights through the institutions of individual private property, contract and the rule of law," and "self-ordering market[s], free trade, free migration, and peace."[28]

As another example, the John M. Olin Institute for Strategic Studies, a unit of Harvard University's Center for International Affairs, was funded by the Olin and Scaife foundations and corporations such as Northrop—the large defense contractor—that stand to benefit if the center's hawkish defense views become government policy.[29]

Few of the dollars coming into most on-campus think tanks, however, are spent on students. The Hoover Institution spent 60 percent of its budget on research and publications, 33 percent on its libraries, and 7 percent on administration.[30] Harvard University's Center for International Affairs had an income of $3,996,052 and expenses of $3,977,269 in 1991. Of these expenditures, $33,040 (or less than 1 percent) was spent on student programs. By contrast, $2,878,973 (or 72 percent) was spent on research programs and $625,995 (or 16 percent) was spent on administration.[31]

When money does go to students, as it does at George Mason's Institute for Humane Studies (IHS), it is typically awarded to students who have demonstrated an affinity for the "free market" values that these think tanks espouse. For example, the IHS-Eberhard Award goes to the law student who "best analyzes a case or legal topic of interest to conservatives and libertarians." The IHS-Felix Morley Award is given to a journalism student who has published "editorials, op-eds, articles, essays, and reviews that reflect the classical principles of individual liberty and free markets." Not a nickel is available from the IHS for students who write about the inequities associated with corporate capitalism.[32]

While administrators invite these ideologically motivated research centers to their universities to get money, many professors join them to get promoted. The think tanks sponsor numerous conferences and churn out pamphlets and journals. These publications of think tanks, rather than traditional academic journals, bloat the résumés of many professors. For example, H. Joachim Maitre, the former dean of Boston University's College of Communication discussed in Chapter Two, built his career by writing for think-tank publications such as *Defense Media Review* (issued by BU's Center for Defense Journalism), rather than for traditional scholarly journals. Maitre heads the center, and his byline can be found in almost every issue of the *Review*.

Think Tanks for Laissez-Faire Domestic Policy

There are think tanks at universities that conduct bona fide policy research, and some even tilt a bit to the left, but many on-campus think tanks are propaganda mills rather than research laboratories. These "advocacy tanks" are found at public and private, large and small universities around the country. Some—including George Mason, Boston, and Texas A&M universities—have several conservative centers on campus. For example, Texas A&M has one think tank devoted to economic and domestic issues—the Center for Education and Research in Free Enterprise—and another devoted to defense and foreign policy issues—the Mosher Institute for International Policy. The Center for Education and Research in Free Enterprise is headed by an adjunct scholar of the Washington-based Heritage Foundation; the Mosher Institute was headed, until recently, by a former Air Force colonel and Reagan administration official.

Most conservative advocacy tanks, like the Center for Education and Research in Free Enterprise at Texas A&M, claim to be nonpartisan, scholarly enterprises, but instead produce highly politicized reports, op-ed articles, and soundbites. These think-tank products invariably blame government, rather than corporations, for most of America's social ills. For example, when it came to raising the minimum wage, Texas A&M think-tank head Svetozar Pejovich and other campus think-tank denizens were against it. "It's much better to give people a chance to earn a low wage than to deprive them of the chance to make any wage," Pejovich declared, suggesting that minimum wage laws are unnecessary.[33] Edwin Feulner, Jr., the National Advisory Board chair of the Texas A&M center and president of the Heritage Foundation, declared the Americans with Disabilities Act, the 1990 Clean Air Act amendments, and other government regulations to be "the stake in the economy's heart."[34]

When these think tanks do criticize corporate practices, it is usually because corporate leaders are not as openly right-wing and anti-government as the think tanks are. For example, Clemson University's Center for Policy Studies produced a 400-page report criticizing corporations for donating more money to left-wing than right-wing groups. According to the report, corporations "set aside a portion of their earnings for the benefit of their enemies." It arrived at this illogical conclusion by branding more groups as "left-wing" than Joe McCarthy did in his heyday—including the National Audubon Society, the Trilateral Commission, and the Council on Foreign Relations (which is an elite policy group whose membership chairman at the time was Reagan-Bush national security adviser Brent Scowcroft).[35]

The Center for Study of Public Choice at George Mason University, the leading proponent of "public-choice theory" in the country, masks its right-wing ideology in more sophisticated-sounding economic jargon than the Clemson center does. Like Ronald Reagan's supply-side economists, public-choice theorists argue that government interferes with the correct functioning of the free market and needs to be reduced or eliminated. These shopworn laissez-faire arguments are surrounded with terms and phrases such as "single-peakedness," "the axiom of the independence of irrelevant alternatives," and "rent-seekers"—the last a pejorative term used to describe the beneficiaries of government subsidies.[36]

Many of these think tanks advocating the deregulation of business have Reagan Republicans in residence as guiding gurus. The Center for Study of Public Choice has as its resident Republican James C. Miller III, Reagan's director of the Office of Management and Budget. The Center for the Study of American Business at Washington University in St. Louis is headed by Murray Weidenbaum, Reagan's first chair of the Council of Economic Advisers. And the Bradley Policy Research Center at the University of Rochester is headed by Gregg A. Jarrell, a Reagan-era official whom Bradley center publicity describes as the "principal architect of the Reagan Administration's laissez-faire regulatory policy governing tender offers."[37]

Think Tanks for the Defense Industry

While some think tanks specialize in domestic policy propaganda, others are devoted to serving the military-industrial complex. These centers often have names that sound like the Center for Strategic and International Studies, the conservative, Washington think tank headed by Zbigniew Brzezinski and Henry Kissinger. The on-campus clones of the CSIS include: Center for International Security and Strategic Studies, Mississippi State; Center for National Security Law, University of Virginia at Charlottesville; Center for Defense and Strategic Studies, Southwest Missouri State in Springfield; Institute for Foreign Policy Analysis, Tufts University; Mosher Institute for International Policy Studies, Texas A&M; John M. Olin Institute for Strategic Studies, Harvard University; Institute for the Study of International Terrorism, State University of New York at Oneonta; Center for Defense Journalism, Boston University; Institute for the Study of Ideology, Conflict and Policy, Boston University; Center for International Studies, University of St. Thomas in Houston; and James Baker III Institute for Public Policy at Rice University in Houston.

All these think tanks report that their purpose is to conduct detached research concerning national security and defense issues. For example, the Center for National Security Law at the University of Virginia at Charlottesville reports that it produces "non-partisan, interdisciplinary advanced research and scholarship concerning the interaction between U.S. and international law and the national security and foreign policy interests of the nation."[38] In reality, it produces highly partisan, hawkish propaganda tracts that urge "continued vigilance" against narco-terrorists and radical regimes, and "continuing investment" in intelligence gathering and weaponry.[39]

"Scholars" at these institutes are invariably conservatives who have close ties to the defense establishment and Republican Party. John Norton Moore and Robert F. Turner, the director and the associate director of the Center for National Security Law, held appointments with the Reagan administration. Robert L. Pfaltzgraff, Jr., president of the Tufts-affiliated Institute of Foreign Policy Analysis, describes himself as a government adviser on "military strategy, modernization, and arms control policy" and a "consultant to industry clients."[40]

Not only do these think-tank scholars have political and defense industry ties, but much of the money used to finance think-tank operations comes from defense contractors and from foundations, like the Lynde and Harry Bradley Foundation, that were established by defense contractors. For example, the Institute for Foreign Policy Analysis has recieved money from the Bradley Foundation, Rockwell International and the Raytheon Company's Missile Division. After receiving the Raytheon money, IFPA president Robert Pfaltzgraff, in a *Wall Street Journal* op-ed article, defended Raytheon's patriot missile from criticism that it failed to intercept incoming missiles during the Gulf War.[41] Pfaltzgraff's op-ed byline failed to mention his IFPA ties or Raytheon's funding of the think tank.

Despite their political and industry ties, the university affiliations of these think tanks give them an aura of objectivity and thus a credibility that overtly partisan think tanks lack. They use their aura of objectivity to influence public opinion by producing op-ed articles, volunteering for soundbites, publishing journals and books, and sponsoring highly publicized forums, where conservative speakers always outnumber liberals.

Several on-campus think-tank denizens—such as Robert F. Turner and Ron Hatchett, former director of Texas A&M's Mosher Institute for International Studies and current head of the Center for International Studies at the University of St. Thomas in Houston—are prolific producers of op-eds. For example, during the Gulf War, Turner penned op-eds for the *Washington Post* and *Christian Science Monitor* criticizing advocates of a negotiated peace and justifying the assassination of Saddam Hussein. The op-ed bylines identified Turner as a professor and "associate director of the Center for National Security Law at the University of Virginia, Charlottesville," not as a former Reagan-Bush administration official.[42] Hatchett, another ex-Reagan administration official, writes op-eds with such alarmist titles as "Soviet Union Dead—Red Army Alive" and "Get Ready for the Worst Coming Out of Russia." His op-eds usually describe him as a university-based scholar rather than as a former official, too.[43]

The type of "scholarly" publication that these think tanks produce is exemplified by *Propaganda Disinformation Persuasion*, a quarterly journal published by BU's Disinformation Documentation Center. The center and the Program for the Study of Disinformation are headed by Ladislav Bittman, a former Czechoslovak intelligence agent, who is also editor of the journal. Its spring 1991 issue, published six years after Mikhail Gorbachev came to power and four years after Ronald Reagan declared the Cold War over, echoed the paranoia of fifties-era anti-communism:

> In accordance with the principles of Gorbachev's new thinking, the Soviet Union seeks to install pro-Soviet lobbyists in the economic and political structures of Western societies. Active measures and disinformation about the real goals of the unchanged Communist Party elite's interests play one of the major roles in achieving this end.[44]

However, rather than exposing the ideological content and corporate funding of this research produced at on-campus think tanks, news reporters instead turn repeatedly to think-tank denizens for soundbites and quotes. Yonah Alexander, head of the Institute for the Study of International Terrorism at SUNY at Oneonta,[45] has been quoted several hundred times by the news media; Robert F. Turner and Robert Pfaltzgraff have been quoted by the *Washington*

Post, Boston Globe, and other newspapers. "Scholars" at the Hoover Institution have been quoted thousands of times by reporters for the *New York Times, Chicago Tribune, Los Angeles Times,* television networks, and other media, which helps explain why the issue of "political correctness" became a media issue so quickly in the early 1990s—the denizens helped put it on the agenda.[46]

Think Tanks: Boosters of Corporate and Conservative Ideology

Think tanks, particularly those with pro-corporate or politically conservative agendas, have been taking root on college campuses, just as they have been in cities around the United States. These think tanks include:

- The John M. Ashbrook Center for Public Affairs, Ashland University in Ashland, Ohio
- Karl Eller Center for the Study of the Private Market Economy, University of Arizona
- Institute for the Study of Economic Culture, Boston University
- Social Philosophy and Policy Center, Bowling Green State University
- Olin Center for Policy, University of California at Los Angeles
- Center for the Study of the Economy and the State, University of Chicago
- Olin Center for Inquiry into the Theory and Practice of Democracy, University of Chicago
- Henry Salvatori Center for the Study of Individual Freedom, Claremont McKenna College in Claremont, California
- Center for Policy Studies, Clemson University
- Center for the Study of Public Choice, George Mason University
- Institute for Humane Studies, George Mason University
- Center for the Study of Market Processes, George Mason University
- Shavano Institute/Center for Constructive Alternatives, Hillsdale College in Hillsdale, Michigan
- Institute for American Values, Nichols College in Dudley, Massachusetts
- Bradley Policy Research Center, University of Rochester
- Center for the Study of Social and Political Change, Smith College
- Economic Enterprise Institute, University of South Carolina
- Center for Education and Research in Free Enterprise, Texas A&M
- Center for Economic Education, University of Tennessee at Chatanooga
- Center for the Study of American Business, Washington University

Chapter Eight

Servicing Their Patrons

Universities first established endowed professorships or "chairs" to honor nationally known scholars who taught at or graduated from them. Either the university or alumni funded the endowed positions in the hopes of motivating others to follow in the footsteps of distinguished scholars. For example, Harvard University's Charles Eliot Norton Professorship of Poetry honors the university's first professor of the history of art, who retired in 1898. Harvard also houses the Samuel Hazard Cross Professorship of Slavic Languages, named for a distinguished Harvard professor who died of a heart attack at age fifty-five.

Other endowed professorships are named for deceased alumni who willed their estates to their alma maters. For example, in 1991, Gretchen Colnik, a Marquette University alumna and Milwaukee television celebrity, bequeathed her estate to Marquette to establish the Gretchen and Cyril Colnik Chair of Communication. In 1970, Alice Burbank bequeathed $1.2 million to Harvard to establish the Burbank Professorship of Political Economy in the name of her late husband, Harold, who had been an economics professor there for nearly 40 years.

Increasingly, however, endowed chairs are funded by and named for corporations, conservative foundations, right-wing politicians, and breathing fat cats, rather than deceased alumni or scholars. These donors usually contribute to universities out of vanity (which is why the endowed professorships bear the tycoons' names), or to further their corporations' economic or political interests.[1] Contributions made to universities to endow professorships are tax-deductible, even when the professorships further a particular economic or political agenda. One example is the Reliance Professorship of Private Enterprise at the University of Pennsylvania. The initial agreement between Penn and Saul Steinberg, the president of Reliance Corp., specified that the professor holding the endowed chair would "be a spokesperson for the free enterprise system" and engage "twice a year in employee training or another aspect of Reliance operations."[2]

Another example is the professorships in "the Economics of the Defense Industrial Base" endowed by General Dynamics for the U.S. Air Force, Military, and Naval academies. In 1993, General Dynamics announced that it was donating $1.5 million to endow the professorships so that future military leaders would learn the need to preserve the "defense industrial base."[3] The positions were clearly marked for professors who would advocate spending for military hardware.

Other professorships endowed to further corporate or political agendas have names such as the Bell South Professor of Education through Telecommunication (at the University of South Carolina), the Ronald Reagan Chair of Broadcasting (at the University of Alabama), the John G. McCoy-Banc One Corp. Professor of Creativity and Innovation (at Stanford University), Fuyo Bank Professorship of Japanese Law (at Columbia University), and the Lamar Savings Professor of Finance (at Texas A&M University). This last professorship is named for a defunct savings and loan whose operators were convicted of embezzling $85 million.[4]

When tycoons or corporations fund professorships, they usually write a description of the responsibilities and attributes of the chaired professors. For example, Harvard's Eaton Professorship requires the holder to be "an able and patriotic citizen" who is devoted to "the great principles upon which our national constitution is based." (No anarchists need apply for this position!) Another Harvard position, the Carl A. Pescosolido Professorship (which is named for and funded by an Italian-American oil magnate), was created "to teach Americans the tremendous importance, though in our times quite subtle, of Ancient Rome and Italy to our present Western culture." As an example from outside Harvard, a law professorship at DePaul University in Chicago was endowed by attorney Robert A. Clifford to counter the "well-funded machine of the

insurance industry and the medical societies" that exagg
impact of malpractice suits brought by "tasseled-loafer la ,⸜ers on
health costs. (Upon endowing the professorship, Clifford, who is
also a DePaul University trustee, said, "I'm a tasseled-loafer lawyer
and I'm proud of it."[5])

These professorships are often of questionable academic value.
One such position at the University of Minnesota provides a good
example. Travel tycoon Curt Carlson owns the Carlson Travel Network, which is the university's preferred travel agency despite com-
plaints that "Carlson doesn't do enough to find [faculty] the lowest
air fare."[6] In 1991, Carlson endowed the nation's first chaired professorship in tourism, called the Carlson Travel, Tourism and Hos-
pitality Chair, at the university. When the chaired professorship
was publicly announced, a university spokesperson unabashedly
proclaimed that the travel "industry needs research and education
like any other...academic area of inquiry."[7] The comment reveals
the thinking among many administrators and university fund raisers that industrial R&D and academic inquiry are synonymous.

The Executives' Chairs

Universities sell funded professorships for money. The salaries
of endowed professors are picked up entirely or partly by the endowment, and this underwriting means that university money
originally earmarked for salaries can be used for other purposes.
University administrators sometimes use these extra funds for enter-
taining, travel, and even home remodeling, as noted in Chapter Two.

The corporate endowments allow universities to pay professors
with endowed chairs more than other professors. At UCLA, regular
full professors earn a top salary of $91,300 in liberal arts depart-
ments and $100,300 in the business school.[8] Holders of endowed
chairs are paid significantly more. In 1993-94, the Allstate Chair
was paid $129,000, the IBM Chair was paid $109,400, the Times
Mirror Chair was paid $125,000, and the Medberry Chair was paid
$118,000.

Like most highly paid professors, holders of endowed professorships usually teach less than their lower-paid colleagues. For example, James Q. Wilson, the James A. Collins Chair in
Management at UCLA's business school, teaches just three classes

per year. The classes have such titles as "The Morality of Capitalism" and "The Political Environment of U.S. Business."[9] Wilson, a guru of the neoconservative movement who has a Ph.D. in political science, not business, received $120,000 in salary during 1993-94. His diminutive teaching responsibilities explain how he has had time to write numerous books, book reviews, and articles on violent crime, abortion, and President Clinton for conservative publications such as *Commentary* and *The Public Interest*.

Moreover, universities are obliged by their corporate funders to fill endowed professorships with individuals like Wilson, whom corporate contributors find acceptable. These are usually corporate cheerleaders, political conservatives, or deregulation advocates such as Sam Peltzman, the Sears Roebuck Professor of Economics at the University of Chicago. Peltzman is a vociferous opponent of business regulation and a former staff economist with President Nixon's Council of Economic Advisers.[10] Similarly, at Florida State University in Tallahassee, the McKenzie Professor of Government and Policy Sciences, named for a Florida trucking magnate, is Thomas Dye, an ardent opponent of "antigrowth" taxes, such as state income taxes, and a board member of the James Madison Institute, a right-wing think tank.[11]

Universities actively solicit funds for endowed professorships such as these and produce brochures that tell potential funders how to endow positions—and the cost of each type. For example, Johns Hopkins University's brochure reports that it wants $2 million for "distinguished university professorships" and $1.5 million for "full professorships." The brochure states that "an endowed Deanship for a school is a particular honor. The funding required is more than $2 million."[12] As another example, Duke University charges about the same as Johns Hopkins for a distinguished professorship—about $1.5 million. Some of the distinguished professors established at Duke include the Burlington Industries Professorship, the Distinguished Bank Research Professorship, the Hanes Corporation Foundation Professorship, and the ITT/Terry Sanford Professorship.[13]

Public universities such as the University of North Carolina hawk professorships for less money than these private universities. For instance, North Carolina's most expensive professorship can be endowed for $1 million, half of what it costs to endow a position at

Johns Hopkins. It also sells a bottom-of-the-line "Named Distinguished Professorship" for $500,000. And the University of Texas sells its professorships for even less, but it also houses more endowed positions than any other university. By 1991, the University of Texas at Austin had 1,051 endowed chairs, endowed professorships, and endowed faculty fellowships.[14]

It's not hard to see the reason for this soliciting. These endowed chairs show that university administrators are bringing outside funding to their universities. Thus, alumni magazines and newsletters always run stories about endowed chairs to encourage other alumni to endow professorships. For example, the June 1994 issue of *Michigan Today*, the alumni newspaper of the University of Michigan, carried an article about endowed professorships with the headline, "Seats of Learning: Endowed Chairs Are the Base of University's Intellectual Life." Accompanying this story was another about the university's fund-raising campaign, which sought to raise $190 million for the "endowment of professorships"—but just $125 million for student scholarships and fellowships.

Harvard University also touts its endowed professorships. The university published a book titled *Harvard University History of Named Chairs: Sketches of Donors and Donations* that fund raisers give to wealthy patrons whom they are courting. The gold-embossed book provides embarrassingly sycophantic biographies of donors, which suggest to potential donors that Harvard is willing to whitewash their records—for a large contribution. For example, Aga Khan III, who endowed the Aga Khan Professorship of Iranian, is described as having been "acquainted with most of the royal families. He traveled extensively. He informed himself on a multitude of subjects and became one of the most influential leaders of the Muslim world. He was a founder and first president of the All-India Muslim League. He worked assiduously and generously to build Aligraph University into a great Muslim institution."[15] This biography neglects to mention that Aga Khan, a religious and political leader, squandered his subjects' money on race horses and collaborated with Britain to maintain colonial rule in India.

When a corporation or tycoon funds a professorship, university public relations departments work overtime to get the funding covered by newspapers, which can reach alumni who are not on the university's mailing list. In this way, the corporation or tycoon gets good press and the university attracts more donors. For example, when the San Paolo Chair of International Journalism was established at Columbia University's Graduate School of Journalism, Columbia sent out a press release. The *New York Times* dutifully carried a fawning article about the San Paolo Chair and Furio Colombo, who was appointed to the chair. The *Times* reported:

> The author, professor, journalist, television producer and businessman Furio Colombo added yet another facet to his career as the new San Paulo Professor of International Journalism at Columbia...The chair was established last week with a grant from the San Paolo Foundation, the philanthropic entity of a Turin-based bank.[16]

However, there was another angle on this story that the *Times* neglected. In this case, the endowed chair was actually established at the urging of the "scholar" who filled the position. The chair was endowed by the Turin-based bank at the urging of Colombo, who chairs the public relations wing of Fiat, a company that virtually runs Turin. "It was Furio Colombo's wish that we set up this professorship in international journalism," said Luizella Giorda, the head of the bank's international division.[17]

One explanation for why the *New York Times* missed the real story about the San Paulo Chair is that information provided about the appointment by Columbia administrators was either accidently erroneous or intentionally misleading. Joan Konner, dean of the journalism school, who reportedly lobbied for Colombo's appointment, contends that "there were definitely other candidates" besides him. Colombo was selected for the position because of his outstanding credentials, Konner contended. She described Colombo as "a recognized journalist. We checked his credentials with American and Italian journalists and found out he is indeed considered a fine journalist with a long list of credentials."[18]

However, Karen Rothmyer, a former Columbia journalism professor who resigned from the committee that searched for the San Paulo Professor, said that "as far as I was ever told or heard, there was never any other candidate" except Colombo. Professor Phyllis Garland, another Columbia journalism professor, said that Colombo's name was given to the search committee, not generated by it. She contended that Colombo "was a present to us. The money did not come from our budget, and he filled a position that we had not established. If we had established the position, we would have advertised. But there was no advertising for this position. He came by a different avenue."[19]

As for Colombo's credentials as a journalist, Giorgio Bocca, a columnist for *L'Espresso*, described him as "more a businessman or a high-level P.R. man than he is a journalist. He is an ambassador for the Agnelli family [which owns Fiat], and he spends much of his time on that." Gay Talese (a friend of Colombo's, along with Gerald Ford and Henry Kissinger) described him as "a prince of sorts to [the Agnelli] court, a cultural prince, a cultural attache."[20] In effect, Columbia's journalism school put a PR man on its faculty for $1.8 million.

The San Paolo Professor of International Journalism is just one of many endowed professorships funded by foreign governments, corporations, and foundations. At MIT, for example, Japanese corporations such as Mitsubishi and Mitsui have endowed 16 chairs. At Johns Hopkins University, the Japan Shipbuilding Foundation endowed a chair in the name of former Japanese Premier Yasuhiro Nakasone, who headed a bribery- and influence-peddling-infested administration. However, universities are not influenced by such funding, says Johns Hopkins dean George R. Packard. "We are uninfluenced by Japanese money," Packard claims.[21]

A different view of such funding is given by John Yochelson at the Center for Strategic and International Studies, a conservative think tank in Washington that also has an endowed chair funded by Japan. "We aren't going to bend over backward to put a Japan-basher in the chair," Yochelson admits. Former Commerce Department trade negotiator Clyde Prestowitz also suggests that recipients of Japanese money do their best not to irritate their patrons. "You shine your shoes because you anticipate he [the patron] would like your shoes shined, not because he tells you to shine your shoes," Prestowitz explains.[22]

The Free Enterprise Chairs

In addition to the named professorships, corporations and right-wing donors have funded nearly 100 "free enterprise chairs" over the last decade and a half. (See sidebar for examples.) These chairs differ from other endowed chairs because they are politically, rather than just economically, motivated. The free enterprise chairs were funded because many corporations felt that universities had not been providing sufficient instruction in "traditional American values." The free enterprise chairs champion the need for a marketplace where businesses are free from government regulations.[23]

"The purpose of the free enterprise chairs is ideological. Their purpose is to assure that a pro-business perspective is presented," says Edward Herman, a professor at the University of Pennsylvania and a critic of funded chairs. Because businesses have the money to fund chairs and other groups do not, only one side is represented by these endowed professorships, Herman contends.[24]

Herman's analysis is supported by Michael Mescon, the former dean of Georgia State University's (GSU) business school and holder of the Ramsey Chair of Private Enterprise, the first endowed chair of its type in the country. Mescon admits that the chairs are ideologically motivated, and this motivation explains why they are named "free enterprise" chairs. "Everything you do, you do right on top of the table and in broad daylight," Mescon says.[25] (Mescon retired from GSU in 1989 and became a full-time consultant.)

At many universities with free enterprise chairs, there are also parallel programs or endowments that countenance conservativism. For example, Trinity College in Connecticut houses the Shelby Cullom Davis Chair of American Business and Economic Enterprise, named for the financier who is chair of the Heritage Foundation's board of trustees. Trinity also houses the Shelby Cullom Davis Endowment, which funds campus events such as a symposium on "educational challenges" that was co-sponsored with the Yankee Institute, an off-campus, right-wing think tank.[26] In this way, tycoon and corporate dollars not only buy professorships, but are also able to dominate the campus ideological environment.

With big money, even a single person can influence the political environment on campus. Junk-bond dealer and takeover artist Saul Steinberg not only funded the Reliance Professorship of Management and Private Enterprise at the University of Pennsylvania, but as a university trustee, he has had a major influence on university programs. He has funded several other events at Penn, such as

Examples Of Free Enterprise Chairs

University	Free Enterprise Chair
Baylor University	Mays Professorship
Georgia State University	Georgia-Cobb Chair
Kent State University	Goodyear Professorship
Loyola (Chicago)	Marotta Professorship
Memphis State	Chair of Excellence
Middle Tennessee State	Jones Chair
Ohio State University	Davis Professorship
Purdue University	Morgan Professorship
Texas A&M	Grey Professorship
Trinity College	Davis Professorship
Troy State University	Bibby Chair
University of Akron	Goodyear Chair
University of California at Irvine	Gerken Professorship
University of Georgia	Ramsey Professorship
University of Miami	McLamore/Burger King Chair
University of Mississippi	Herrin-Hess Professorship
University of Tampa	Hollingsworth Chair
University of Tennessee (Chattanooga)	Probasco Professorship
University of Tennessee (Martin)	Hendrix Professorship
University of Virginia	Beeton Professorship
University of Texas (Austin)	Bayless/Farish Chair
Washington and Jefferson College	Hardy Professorship

the Steinberg Memorial Lectures program, which brings notable speakers to campus. The Steinberg speakers included a few international personages such as Turkish president Turgat Ozal, but the majority have been conservative luminaries—such as American Enterprise Institute fellow Michael Novak and U.S. Secretary of Defense Dick Cheney—or free market entrepreneurs—such as professor-turned-management consultant Peter Drucker.[27]

The majority of free enterprise chairs are found at southern universities and smaller colleges, but many large universities outside the South also have such chairs. Purdue University, for example, has the Burton Morgan Professorship for the Study of Private Enterprise, which is named for an alumnus who owns an adhesives factory. And Kent State University in Kent, Ohio has the Goodyear Professorship of Free Enterprise, which was funded by Goodyear Tire and Rubber. According to Chris Welles, the former business editor of the *Saturday Evening Post* and *Life* magazine, the Goodyear professorship was first "occupied by a retired advertising executive, who regard[ed] the job as an opportunity to serve as a 'business missionary.'" (Welles's statement was made at a symposium at the University of Missouri at Columbia that was funded by ITT.)[28]

Although these free enterprise chairs are funded by different tycoons and corporations, professors who hold these chairs are part of a broad network linking on-campus research centers and right-wing Washington think tanks (like the American Enterprise Institute, Heritage Foundation, and Cato Institute) whose purpose is to produce and distribute pro-corporate propaganda, rather than to teach or conduct bona fide research. When think tanks quote materials written by professors bearing important-sounding titles such as the "Gerken Professor of Enterprise and Society at the University of California-Irvine," it makes their propaganda more persuasive (see Chapter Seven).

This free enterprise network has both formal and informal aspects. The backbone of the formal network is the Association of Private Enterprise Education, which was established in 1978 to "promote an accurate understanding of the American economic system through teaching, research, and communication between academe and business."[29] The "accurate understanding" that the association seeks to promote is actually the ideologically conservative view that government regulation of business is harmful to the public. Dwight Lee, the Ramsey Professor of Economics and Private Enterprise at the University of Georgia, summed the view up in an article criticizing Democratic Party proposals to extend worker benefits. Lee wrote:

> [President] Clinton has promised to increase the number of mandated benefits businesses are required to provide to their workers...In addition to family leave, Clinton has promised legislation mandating health insurance, increasing the minimum wage...and requiring that 1.5 percent of a company's payroll be spent on training for its employees. Despite the best intentions, and superficial appearances, such mandated benefits reduce the well-being of all workers.[30]

The Association of Private Enterprise Education is headquartered at the University of Tennessee at Martin, which houses the Tom E. Hendrix Chair of Excellence in Free Enterprise, and it publishes two impressive-sounding propaganda journals, *Journal of Private Enterprise* and *Enterprise and Education. Enterprise and Education* is distributed free to anyone willing to take it.

The informal network is created by a host of campus-based free enterprise centers and programs, which have large budgets to bring other free marketeers onto campuses for conferences, colloquia, and speeches. The most frequent speakers at these events are well-known conservatives such as William F. Buckley, Jr., Irving Kristol, and Michael Novak.

Another part of the informal network consists of the joint appointments held by free enterprise chair holders. Frequently, a free enterprise chair holder at one university will get an adjunct appointment with a free enterprise center at another university or think tank, giving the holder an array of titles that dazzle colleagues, the public, and the press. Multiple titles give free enterprise savants the appearance of erudition, which boosts their credibility, making them more likely to be quoted as "experts" by news reporters.[31]

The titles that Jordan's King Hussein holds—King, Commander in Chief, head of state, and upholder of the faith—are dwarfed by some professors' titles. For example, Dwight Lee, the Ramsey Chaired Professor of Economics and Private Enterprise at the University of Georgia, is an adjunct scholar at George Mason

University's Center for the Study of Public Choice and a visiting scholar at Washington University's Center for the Study of American Business. Thomas DiLorenzo, the Scott L. Probasco Professor of Free Enterprise, is also director of the Center for Economic Education at the University of Tennessee in Chattanooga, a "resident scholar" at Washington University's Center for the Study of American Business, and an adjunct scholar at the Cato Institute. Richard B. McKenzie, the Gerken Professor of Enterprise and Society at the University of California at Irvine, is also the John M. Olin adjunct professor at Washington University's Center for the Study of American Business. McKenzie, like other free enterprise chairs, has ties with numerous on- and off-campus think tanks. For example, his books have been published and distributed by the Hoover Institution, Heritage Foundation, Cato Institute, and American Enterprise Institute.[32]

Included in this informal network are the professorships funded by the John M. Olin Foundation, such as the one held by McKenzie at Washington University. These professorships and the foundation that bankrolls them demonstrate the multiple ties linking the network together. The John M. Olin Foundation itself was created by a right-wing tycoon who made his fortune in munitions, and its president is William E. Simon, a former Nixon administration official and ultrarightist who has repeatedly stated that his "philanthropy" is ideologically motivated. Simon wrote that corporate chiefs must steer corporate and foundation gifts to pro-business groups and individuals. "Naturally, this idea is criticized by collectivists who have an obvious interest in shooting down the notion that donors ought to have any say as to who gets their money and what they do with it."[33]

The Olin Foundation has endowed professorships at a dozen universities, including Carnegie-Mellon University in Pittsburgh, Pennsylvania, George Mason, Yale, Georgetown, New York University, and Fordham University in New York City. The Olin professorships are usually earmarked for former Republican officials and political conservatives with close ties to right-wing think tanks. The Olin Professor of Political Economy and Public Policy at Carnegie-Mellon is Allan Meltzer, who was an economic adviser to the Reagan and Bush administrations and a former American Enterprise

Institute fellow. The Olin Professor at George Mason is Walter E. Williams, who argues that poverty among Blacks stems primarily from interference in the free market by government and labor unions. He is a former Heritage Foundation fellow.

Other Olin professors include George Priest, Olin Professor of Law at Yale University, who was a member of President Reagan's Commission on Privatization; Walter Berns, Olin University Professor at Georgetown University, who is an adjunct scholar at the American Enterprise Institute; Herbert London, Olin Professor of Humanities at New York University, who co-founded the National Association of Scholars; Ernest van der Haag, Olin Professor of Jurisprudence and Public Policy *emeritus*, who is a "distinguished scholar" at the Heritage Foundation and contributing editor to the *National Review*; and Irving Kristol, who was the Olin Distinguished Professor of Social Thought at NYU.

Paying for Programs of Study

Corporations and foundations can also strengthen their ties to universities by funding not just individual chairs, but entire programs of study. For example, in addition to funding professorships, the Olin Foundation gives money for such programs of study as the academically questionable field of "Law and Economics." (See sidebar on George Mason University's Law and Economics program.) "Law and Economics" is the application of extremist laissez-faire economic philosophy to law. It argues that market forces are superior to government-adopted regulations for establishing legal principles. Proponents of this doctrine want laws and regulations to function as only minor supplements to the marketplace that perfect market mechanisms when needed.[34]

Courses in this ideology-cum-discipline are taught at numerous prestigious law schools, thanks to the Olin Foundation. The foundation funds Law and Economics programs at the University of Chicago, Yale, Stanford, Harvard, Columbia, George Mason, Georgetown, Duke, Penn, and the University of Virginia. The programs provide fellowships to law students at these universities.

The foundation has required students receiving its fellowships to attend Law and Economics seminars, and sometimes has even paid students to enroll in the program. A short-lived program in

The Mecca of Law and Economics

Compared to George Mason University, the law schools at Columbia, Harvard, Georgetown, and Stanford merely dabble in Law and Economics. Henry Manne, dean of George Mason's law school, has made Law and Economics the official theology of his fiefdom, and even has led an inquisition against heretics.

George Mason University president George Johnson, who has close ties to businesspeople and prominent Fairfax County Republicans, brought Manne and the Law and Economics Center to his university in 1986. With a mandate from Johnson, Manne revamped the law school curriculum and started replacing the faculty of the law school.

Manne made Law and Economics the dominant philosophy by hiring professors with solid conservative credentials and forcing out other professors. He reportedly pressured two tenured faculty members to resign and blocked the tenure of a third, who was recommended for tenure by a faculty committee. Within two years, Manne hired 11 new professors in a school with 25 faculty. His hires included Peter Ferrara, a former Reagan White House senior staff member; Lee Liberman, a former special assistant to Antonin Scalia; and Timothy Muris, a Republican political appointee who served as executive associate director of the Office of Management and Budget. As adjunct professors, Manne hired rejected Supreme Court nominees Robert Bork and Douglas Ginsberg. One professor described Manne's actions as "a hostile takeover of the law school."[35]

The curriculum was also revamped to make sure that students got a healthy—or perhaps unhealthy—dose of Law and Economics courses. Traditional law-school courses were scaled back because they fostered a "trade school mentality," and courses such as "Quantitative Methods for Lawyers" (which teaches the fundamentals of economics, finance, and statistics) were made requirements. Manne also decided that the law review was no longer to be edited by students, a move protested by numerous law students.[36]

Manne's Law and Economics crusade was made possible by hefty grants from the Olin, Bradley, Sarah Scaife, and Smith Richardson foundations, which poured approximately three-quarters-of-a-million dollars into the law school between 1988 and 1992. The grants provided money for course development and faculty research, but also helped fund seminars for federal judges. The foundation monies are augmented by corporate dollars from Exxon, ITT, General Motors, Bethlehem Steel, and other business behemoths.

The judicial seminars are technically run by the Law and Economics Center, which is operated by Manne. Manne founded the center when he was at the University of Miami, moved it to Emory University, where he briefly taught, and then transported it to George Mason when he became dean there. The center conducts one- and two-week-long seminars for federal judges that deal with economics as interpreted by Manne and his antiregulation followers. Classes are offered on "How Competitive Markets Work" and "The Modern Corporation." To make the seminars attractive, they are offered at resort locations such as Naples and Marco Island, Florida. More than 40 percent of federal judges have attended the seminars, with the center typically picking up their tab.

The Alliance for Justice has criticized the judicial seminars as "conservative efforts to influence the legal system."[37] Manne rejects this criticism, using language reminiscent of Stalinist claims to "scientific socialism." Manne claims, "Basic economic theory of prices, of markets, private property, of the exchange of property—these things are substantially at the level of a scientific approach. There is general agreement basic economics is all the same."[38]

However, Judge Jack Weinstein of New York, who has attended the seminars, says, "I think that the Manne seminars are more oriented toward a conservative view of economics by the people they choose and by the nature of the curriculum." Judge Weinstein states that as a result of attending the seminars, "I'm much more prone to accept an economic view and analysis of jurisprudence, and much more prone to accept the market system as a mediator rather than a controlled, bureaucratic model."[39]

Law and Economics was offered at UCLA during the 1980s, but was abandoned after a curriculum committee found that the program was "taking advantage of students' financial need to indoctrinate them with a particular ideology." The program required students receiving Olin fellowships to attend the Olin Symposium in Law and Economics, where a host of right-wing ideologues, including Supreme Court Justice Antonin Scalia and rejected Supreme Court nominee Robert Bork, expounded on their philosophies of justice.[40]

Although UCLA rejected the Law and Economics program because the program took advantage of students' financial need, other universities have not done so. Georgetown University, for example, received Olin grants of about a half-million dollars between 1989 and 1993, with a large amount of the money earmarked for Law and Economics. The grants included $60,000 for a Law and Economics seminar, in which students were paid to enroll. According to a report issued by the public interest group the Alliance for Justice,

> Students are accepted into the seminar at the discretion of the professors. This format is different from that pertaining to most Georgetown seminars in which enrollment is generally based on availability and seniority. Currently, selected students are awarded $4,000 a year *and* receive course credit, a feature unlike that offered for any other course at Georgetown.[41]

The seminar also runs a full year, rather than a single semester, and awards a $2,000 prize to the student who writes the best paper.

Other universities receiving Olin Foundation money also provide incentives for students to enroll in Law and Economics courses. At Harvard, students are paid to attend the courses. At the University of Chicago, the institution that founded the Law and Economics movement, scholarships are given to approximately ten students who "excel academically" but who also must exhibit an interest in Law and Economics. Columbia has made a Law and Economics course a requirement for first-year students.[42]

At Stanford, a range of incentives exist to entice students into Law and Economics. There are research grants and fellowships available to "outstanding students interested in law and economics." There are prizes "to encourage students to excel in law and economics studies." There is even a Law and Economics "free lunch" series, where law students can fill their stomachs while getting an earful of Law and Economics blather. The series is based on the adage that "There is no such thing as a free lunch."[43] The lunch series actually proves the adage—at least when the John M. Olin Foundation is involved.

In addition to enticing students to enroll in Law and Economics courses, the Olin Foundation has had a substantial impact on legal research at universities that receive its "strings-attached" funding. Grants are given to faculty doing Law and Economics research, and this has resulted in an increase in law articles that use Law and Economics as the analytical framework. "In recent years Law and Economics articles have constituted roughly 25% of the scholarship in the Yale, Harvard, Chicago and Stanford law reviews," report Nan Aron, Barbara Moulten and Chris Owens, who are associates of the Alliance for Justice.[44]

The John M. Olin Foundation funds other programs of study—such as a national-security program at Harvard and an international-political-economics program at Duke—but it is not the only well-heeled organization that has bought its way onto campuses and offered classes while there. It is actually very common for businesses to pay for course offerings at business, engineering, and journalism schools. For example, the business journalism program at the University of Missouri at Columbia has been funded by Interstate National Gas Association of America, IBM, Johns-Manville, and Armco Steel.[45] At Gannon University in Erie, Pennsylvania and Springfield College in Springfield, Massachusetts, Hammermill Paper Co. designed and funded courses on economics that were taught to high school teachers. The courses were taught from the perspective of business.[46] Only rarely, as when Newt Gingrich offered a course at Kennesaw State College in Georgia, does this outside funding attract much attention.

In this much-publicized case, House majority leader Newt Gingrich used money from a political action committee, GOPAC, to help fund a course titled "Renewing American Civilization," which he taught in 1993 at Kennesaw.[47] Other funding came from wealthy Republicans and corporations, whose contributions to Gingrich were tax-deductible because they were given through an educational institution, rather than a political party or political action committee. Gingrich actually plugged his corporate donors during lectures. The class was offered to 150 students, who received graduate and undergraduate credit for enrolling.

GOPAC, whose contributors are secret, beamed the course by satellite to other universities and sites around the country. Clemson and Lee universities offered the satellite course to students for credit. Although Gingrich publicly claimed that the course was academic and nonpartisan, the *Atlanta Journal and Constitution* reported that Gingrich hoped that the class would recruit 200,000 conservative workers for the 1996 campaign.[48]

After protests by the Kennesaw political science faculty, who correctly described Gingrich's class as "a political activity, not instruction," the course was moved to Reinhardt College in Waleska, Georgia for the 1994 school year.[49]

If in the future Reinhardt decides not to offer the course, Gingrich will undoubtedly find another college that will. When money is available, it's easy to find a college or university that will sell out academic principles.

Chapter Nine

The Social Costs of Corporate Ties

Corporate, foundation, and tycoon money has had a major, deleterious impact on universities. Financial considerations have altered academic priorities, reduced the importance of teaching, degraded the integrity of academic journals, and determined what research is conducted at universities. The social costs of this influence have been lower-quality education, a reduction in academic freedom, and a covert transfer of resources from the public to the private sector.

Corporate influence has had the greatest impact on university research. Corporations determine what issues university researchers study and whether research findings are publicly reported. Corporate funding has reduced the independence of university researchers, undermining the credibility of reported research results.

Spurred on by corporations, universities encourage professors to abandon classrooms for research centers and laboratories, thereby dramatically reversing university priorities. Universities use research, grant-getting, and corporate contracts, not classroom teaching, as measures of academic performance. Today, successful professors are those who bring in contract and grant money; they are not necessarily good teachers, nor do they necessarily need to even step into the classroom. In fact, the more "successful" a professor is today, the less time she or he will spend teaching. This emphasis on research has reduced the importance and quality of undergraduate instruction while simultaneously boosting tuition costs for students, who are forced to help pay the salaries of professors who never teach.

Professors who cultivate corporate ties get perks, promotion, tenure, and endowed professorships, and move up the university hierarchy. They determine whether other, younger professors will also get promoted and tenured. Thus young professors' academic records are evaluated by full professors, endowed chairs, administrators, and trustees whose criteria for granting tenure are whether the professor has brought in corporate or government grant monies, not whether the professor's scholarship is original or whether she or he is an effective teacher.

As this process continues, more and more tenured faculty at universities will be indentured servants to corporations, rather than independent scholars. The indentured servants will make sure that more of their kind are hired and tenured, and that even fewer free-thinkers are hired. In the end, universities will be as intellectually stimulating as a GM assembly plant.

Although the relationship is not as clear as the one between corporate research and poor undergraduate instruction, corporate investments in universities have had another, more subtle impact on universities. At most campuses, disciplines that cultivate close contacts with industry have large budgets and good facilities. Other disciplines, particularly the arts and humanities, languish in substandard facilities. This not only produces two classes of faculty—the haves and the have-nots—but also two classes of students. Students in the arts and humanities not only receive instruction in shabbier facilities, but are also short-changed because their tuition dollars are diverted to the disciplines that do research for corporations.

Corporate funding has also had a deleterious effect on faculty morale and ethics. The emphasis on contract- and grant-getting at universities, and the two-tier pay system, has reduced the morale of professors in fields—such as literature and fine arts—in which corporations have little interest. Through their actions, university administrators have told professors in these fields that their work and contributions are less valued than the work of professors in areas like business and computer science, which have cultivated close ties with corporations. This lack of respect, in turn, has made professors in these fields place increasing emphasis on "research" and publication, rather than teaching, in the tenure and promotion process. By

146

emphasizing research, professors in literature and the arts have attempted to demonstrate that they are "just as good" as professors of business, medicine, and computer science. This shift in focus has lowered the quality of teaching in these fields, as well.

Perhaps the most striking impact that corporate funding has had on universities has been the influence on professorial ethics. Many professors have cavalierly written off teaching for research, consulting, and expert testimony, even though the academy's primary purpose is to instruct people. Rather than serving these constituents, professors have become servants to their corporate patrons. They eagerly testify on behalf of businesses, publish articles that promote their benefactors' interests, and "massage" research findings so that the findings conform to the sponsors' needs, regardless of what these actions cost the public.

Professors often see little wrong with these actions because the codes governing professors' actions assume that they are independent actors, not corporate puppets. For example, many journals do not require authors to disclose conflicts of interest because they assume that professors answer to their universities, not to an outside sponsor. Leslie Cameron, the director of the American Psychological Association's journals, told me in a 1993 telephone interview that her organization doesn't require authors to disclose conflicts of interest because they rarely arise.[1] When I asked a professor who had received tobacco industry money but had not disclosed this in an article he wrote about tobacco advertising why he had not done so, he explained that "our journals do not require affirmative disclosure," so he had decided not to report the source of his funding.[2]

The Financial Impact of Corporate Research

Since the early 1980s, the largest increase in university expenditures has been for research. At most universities, research expenditures more than doubled between 1980 and 1991. At many large state universities, research expenditures tripled in the same period, as did tuition. As the accompanying table shows (see page 149), research expenditures at the University of Colorado in 1991 were over three times what they were in 1980. At the University of Michigan, research expenditures tripled between 1980 and 1991, whereas instructional expenditures didn't quite double. As a result, Michigan spent nearly as much on research in 1991 as on instruction. Similar increases in research expenditures occurred at large private universities, such as Harvard and MIT, so that their research expenditures now equal or even exceed instructional expenditures.

The primary beneficiaries of these increases in university R&D spending have been corporations, which receive the benefits of the research at a subsidized cost. But it is students and taxpayers who pick up the bill for most of it. At the University of Michigan, for example, corporate grants and contracts during fiscal year 1993 funded about a tenth of the university research, from which corporate interests benefited most. Tuition, federal agencies, state allocations, and university investments paid for the rest. Overall, the university contributed more money to research than did industry.[3]

The research expenditures presented in the accompanying table, and described above, greatly underestimate actual university research expenses because they do not include indirect costs, such as the salaries of university bureaucrats—grants officers, development experts, and lawyers—who secure research contracts and grants. This class of university employee increased more rapidly during the 1980s than any other (see Chapter Two). Other indirect, hidden costs of university research include constructing expensive, state-of-the-art facilities and equipping laboratories. When these hidden costs are added to direct research expenditures, it becomes clear that universities are R&D, not instructional, centers.

Another hidden cost is the increasing diversion of state funds to lure research centers from one university to another. For example, the state of Florida appropriated $66 million to lure a magnet-studying lab from MIT to Florida State University. The lab was brought to Florida in the hopes that it would stimulate more research there and thus bring in additional corporate and government grants.[4] Florida taxpayers will undoubtedly have to pour millions more into the laboratory after it arrives at Florida State.

Another indirect effect of the emphasis on research at universities—one that has contributed to higher tuition and inferior undergraduate instruction—is that universities emphasizing research tend to have expensive, labor-intensive Ph.D. programs, which produce research assistants to work on the R&D projects. At some universities, such as the University of Minnesota, graduate courses are

Expenditures of Major State Universities—Main Campuses (in Millions)

	1980			1991		
	Total	Instruction	Research	Total	Instruction	Research
University of Colorado (Boulder)	$141.9	$39.8	$24.2	$352.5	$111.3	$82.5
University of Florida	$318.3	$106.1	$64.2	$772.7	$229.0	$220.0
University of Georgia	$200.0	$62.1	$39.9	$497.5	$106.6	$130.6
University of Maryland	$183.9	$63.3	$24.4	$524.0	$152.1	$85.6
University of Michigan	$598.4	$153.2	$83.8	$1,759.2	$304.7	$244.4
University of Minnesota	$542.4	$156.3	$85.7	$1,418.9	$329.4	$276.3
University of North Carolina at Chapel Hill	$292.3	$117.4	$44.2	$686.4	$241.1	$103.1
Penn State University	$285.3	$84.3	$40.0	$685.2	$166.1	$179.2
University of Wisconsin (Madison)	$457.4	$111.6	$127.9	$1,188.0	$227.8	$303.1

Source: *American Universities and Colleges*, 12th and 14th editions.

often taught with just two or three Ph.D. students in them. Because professors are teaching these small graduate classes, fewer undergraduate classes are taught, and this scarcity increases the number of students in each undergraduate class.

Sometimes universities hire additional professors to reduce growing class sizes. This strategy simply increases universities' expenditures and thus, ultimately, tuition. Some universities employ graduate students as teaching assistants to provide undergraduate instruction. These teaching assistants, however, usually receive tuition reimbursement, which eliminates tuition dollars that would go to pay professors to teach graduate courses. The professors' salaries must therefore be paid by undergraduates, even though the undergraduate students are not taught by professors.

And when universities face budget cuts, it is undergraduate educational programs, not research laboratories, that face the most draconian cuts. For example, after the state of Wisconsin forced the University of Wisconsin at Milwaukee to trim its budget by $1.85 million, administrators announced that the university would hire more part-time instructors, increase the size of classes, and cut tutorial programs.[5] The university didn't announce any cuts to its research program.

The University of Florida: A Case Study

The University of Florida represents a case study of what has happened at many universities, including the University of Georgia and Penn State. Florida, like other universities, radically increased its expenditures on research, de-emphasized undergraduate teaching, and expanded its Ph.D. programs between 1980 and 1991. In 1980, research expenditures represented 20 percent of Florida's budget; by 1991, research expenditures accounted for 28.5 percent. The budget for research increased from $64.2 million in 1980 to $220 million in 1991.

In contrast, the percentage of the University of Florida's budget that was allocated to instruction actually declined during the same period, dropping from 33.3 to 29.7 percent, even though the amount allocated to education increased.[6] As the percentage of the budget devoted to instruction dropped, so did the amount of time that professors spent teaching. By 1991, only one-fifth of the university's faculty taught four courses per semester, the state-mandated teaching load.[7] Professors were given reduced teaching loads for conducting research and for service-related activities, such as overseeing research centers and laboratories. And Florida has plenty of these, plus a research park that "provides a link between University researchers and industry and is designed to transfer new technologies from the laboratory to the marketplace."[8]

To compensate for the reduced teaching loads, the University of Florida hired new faculty. The UF faculty numbered 2,254 in 1980; in 1991, it numbered 2,900. This growth occurred even though the number of undergraduate students and bachelor's degrees conferred remained constant. In 1980, Florida had 22,908 undergraduate students and conferred 5,040 baccalaureate degrees. In 1991, it had 23,213 undergrad students and conferred 5,005 baccalaureate degrees.

The large increase in the size of Florida's faculty is an outgrowth of the university's research emphasis. As research increased in importance, faculty teaching responsibilities declined. As teaching responsibilities declined, new faculty were hired to teach the classes left behind by professors conducting research.

However, at the University of Florida, as at other universities, the corporate and foundation research dollars flowing into the university did not cover the actual costs of conducting the research. Despite spending $220 million on research in 1991, Florida took in less than half that amount in gifts, contracts, and grants. The difference—and the cost of hiring new professors and funding Ph.D. programs—came from taxpayers and students, whose tuition increased from $742 in 1980 to $1,420 in 1991. (This tuition increase is relatively small compared to many other universities.)

Despite the proportionate drop in instructional expenditures and stagnant undergraduate enrollment, the university added several Ph.D. programs, such as computer science and communications, and actually boosted the number of Ph.D. degrees it confers. These Ph.D. programs produced research and teaching assistants, who assumed some of the duties of research and instruction.

Moving from the Board Room to the Classroom

University research has produced a downward spiral in instructional quality and an upward spiral in tuition at most universities, not just at Florida. The only way that this cycle can be broken is by forcing professors back into classrooms and out of laboratories—by cutting university-corporate ties.

A first step in reversing the downward educational spiral would be the enactment of state laws that require professors at state universities to teach a minimum number of courses (e.g., three) each semester. All professors—including department chairs, endowed professors, and grant-funded researchers—should be required to teach the minimum. This requirement would place more emphasis on teaching, decrease class sizes, and remove the incentive for professors to pursue corporate contracts. It would also make it more likely that teacher-scholars would move into administrative posts, rather than having such posts filled by professional administrators who have little regard for teaching or scholarship.

Another step to reverse this spiral would be to mandate that teaching, not research contracts and grant-getting, be given the greatest weight in the tenure and promotion process. Thus professors who have neglected their classroom responsibilities for consulting, contract research, and other corporate work would be penalized, rather than rewarded.

To accomplish these goals, reformers must change the composition of universities' boards of trustees, which are now dominated by corporate CEOs. Trustees of state universities need to represent their populations, rather than business.[9] One way to accomplish this change in representation would be to enact legislation mandating that these boards of trustees mirror their state's population.

Another step—one that would help reverse the shift of public money to the private sector—would be to change the tax code. City, county, and state governments need to revoke the tax-exempt status of centers, institutes, and laboratories that conduct corporate research at private universities. Because these centers function as corporate R&D laboratories, they should be taxed as though they were corporate, rather than instructional, facilities. The taxes collected from these centers could be used for bona fide educational programs, such as student scholarships.

On a national level, the 1980 University and Small Business Patent Procedures Act needs to be rescinded. It is this law that allows universities to virtually hand over to corporations research funded by taxpayers, providing a major incentive for corporations to cultivate close ties to universities.

Moreover, academic organizations need to change their assumptions, as the American Psychological Association recently did, and require professors to disclose their consulting, contracts, stock ownership, and other conflicts of interest in published research articles. Professors' conflicts of interest should not only be disclosed in articles, but readers should also be warned that the findings are to be viewed as tentative until independently replicated. Academic organizations also need to establish stiff sanctions, such as the expulsion of members who violate their conflict-of-interest rules.

Universities need to adopt similar, but much more strenuous policies, such as prohibiting professors from publishing research in which they have any financial stake. Professors who violate these policies should be fired.

Epilogue

By Jeremy Smith

Center for Campus Organizing

University Conversion Project

When I entered the University of Florida as an undergraduate in 1988, I didn't know what to expect. I was uncertain about my political commitments, doubtful of future economic security, and looking for a way to understand my experience. I wanted college to answer my questions and help me find a place in society.

College life quickly disappointed me. All the clichéd criticisms of U.S. universities I had heard—big classes, indifferent professors—turned out to be true. The classes were large and dehumanizing; the bureaucracy was intolerable; most (though not all) professors were uninterested in teaching undergraduates; and opportunities for debate and exploration were few and far between. The university encouraged us to assemble our résumés and to make business connections—which would help ensure our future economic success, but which served as a poor substitute for education. Moreover, since adequate financial aid was unavailable and tuition climbed every year, I and many other students had to work our ways through school. While perhaps this "built character," it was also exhausting, interfered with our schoolwork, and delayed graduation.

I remember my Yorùbá professor would become frustrated with us, his students, as we were by and large obsessed with grades and not particularly interested in acquiring a thorough knowledge of our academic subjects. We wanted to know just enough to pass the test. He wanted us to engage in our subjects critically and holistically. "You cannot segment knowledge!" he'd exclaim, waving his hands at the note-scribbling students. "Can't seg. know," we'd write, without looking up. Educational institutions had trained us to "segment knowledge" by competing for grades and doing whatever we could to look good on paper. It was training not just for the sake of a smoothly functioning educational system, but for a smooth integration into the corporate workforce, with its similar system of punishment and reward.

The signposts of corporate domination were everywhere on campus. Career expos featured representatives from the largest corporations. Graduate students paid for their educations by working on corporate-sponsored research. Pepsi Cola and Coors beer sponsored campus events. The campus itself was home to several multinational corporations. We rented our videos from the campus Blockbuster video store. We bought our food from the campus Taco Bell, Little Caesars, and Kentucky Fried Chicken. University life was shaped not by the ivory tower, but by the agencies of profit and power.

Decisions that most affected students and educators—tuition increases, program budgets, etc.—were obviously made outside of the university, in collaboration with those more interested in profit than education. Our problems—lack of financial aid, large classes, indifferent professors—which were created by the public decisions of an elite, become our private crosses to bear. Since collective political action was considered "unscholarly" and "irresponsible," students were always looking for the shortcut through the bureaucracy, avoiding the oversized lecture halls by switching into smaller classes, for example. Many of the faculty resolved their lack of personal control by climbing up the hierarchy. It was frustrating and stressful for students and faculty, who blamed each other for these problems rather than the people who were responsible. This feeling of powerlessness was perhaps the most dangerous consequence of the corporatization of our university.

When I graduated in 1994, the Board of Regents was considering a plan to privatize 25% of the state university system, and, for the third time in four years, raise tuition. The state had decided to fund prisons instead of education.

As Lawrence C. Soley makes clear in this book, the corporatization of academia is not an accident or an act of God, but the predictable consequence of decisions made by the men (and the few women) who run economic and political institutions. They have cut federal and state education budgets, shifted budget priorities as dictated by business, and attempted to flatten cultural criticism under the heel of so-called "traditional values." This eloquent, passionate book has a genuinely unfashionable premise: that colleges and universities are declining not because of left-wing "political correctness," but because of right-wing "corporate correctness." Corporate correctness includes the effort not just to enforce the correct ideological line (free markets, Western culture, government by an elite), but to cut many students out of education altogether, by raising the cost of education beyond their reach and erasing their cultural heritage from curricula.

I found the community and intellectual ferment I was looking for when I became a student activist. I found that students and faculty can have a voice in the shape of higher education when they become organized. Many teachers are co-opted by corporations and the government, but I worked with and talked to faculty who resisted the corporatization of education. Some do so passively and quietly; others, such as Dr. David Noble at York University in Toronto, have dedicated their lives to fighting it. I learned how students could level pointed public criticisms, while teachers provided mentorship, research, and continuity from year to year, even if their voices were muted by the threat of a crippled career. After all, students and teachers do share a common interest—the quality of education and life on campus. In order to reclaim higher education, they must act together.

There are many organizations—often underfunded and struggling, but hanging in there—that are fighting against corporate intervention in higher education and U.S. society. Support your local or national organization fighting for democracy in education with either your time or your money. See the next page for a brief list.

—Jeremy Smith
Cambridge, MA
April 1995

A Brief List of Organizations

Black Student Leadership Network
c/o Children's Defense Fund
25 E Street, NW
Washington, DC 20037
(202) 628-8787

An organization that develops leadership and advocacy skills among African-American youth. They publish an excellent series of organizing guides.

Center for Campus Organizing/
University Conversion Project
PO Box 748
Cambridge, MA 02142
(617) 354-9363

Clearinghouse that promotes progressive activism and investigative journalism on campus. Specializes in researching right-wing, corporate, and military involvement on campus. For information on e-mail networks, write to canet-info@pencil.cs.missouri.edu.

Democratic Socialists of America Youth Section
180 Varick Street, 12th floor
New York, NY 10014
(212) 727-8610

The student and youth branch of the nation's largest democratic socialist organization. The campus chapters frequently organize around issues of university democracy and corporate accountability.

Student Environmental Action Coalition
PO Box 10510
Atlanta, GA 30310
(800) 700-SEAC

Activist coalition with hundreds of campus affiliates, with a strong record of combating corporate anti-environmentalism and campus environmental irresponsibility. Publishes a monthly newsletter.

Student Pugwash USA
1638 R Street, NW
Washington, DC 20009
(202) 393-6555

An educational non-profit that investigates the social impact of science and technology.

Teachers for a Democratic Society
PO Box 6405
Evanston, IL 60204
(312) 743-3662

Organization of faculty that promotes discussion of democracy in the curriculum and university.

Unplug
360 Grand Avenue, Box 385
Oakland, CA 94610-4840
(510) 268-1100

Organization working to remove the corporate-sponsored "Channel One" television program from public high schools.

United States Student Association
815 15th Street, NW
Suite 838
Washington, DC 20005
(202) 347-USSA

Organization of student governments committed to progressive politics. Lobbies on behalf of students in Washington, DC.

 Notes

Notes to Chapter One

1. Dinesh D'Souza, "Illiberal Education," *Atlantic Monthly,* March 1991, p. 51.

2. Roger Kimball, *Tenured Radicals* (New York: Harper & Row, 1990), p. xiv.

3. Stephen Balch, Letter to the Editor, *Commentary,* May 1986, p. 15.

4. "Taking Offense," *Newsweek,* December 24, 1990, p. 48.

5. John Taylor, "Are You Politically Correct?" *New York,* January 21, 1991, p. 40.

6. James W. Carey, "The Academy and Its Discontents," *Gannett Center Journal,* Spring-Summer 1991, p. 169.

7. Roger Kimball, "The Tyranny of Virtue," *Gannett Center Journal,* Spring-Summer 1991, p. 155.

8. John Taylor, *New York, op. cit.,* p. 35; Roger Kimball, *Tenured Radicals, op. cit.,* p. xvi; Dinesh D'Souza, *Illiberal Education* (New York: The Free Press, 1991), pp. 9-10; Stephen Chapman, "Campus Speech Codes Are on the Way to Extinction," *Chicago Tribune,* July 9, 1992, p. 21.

9. Martin Anderson, *Impostors in the Temple* (New York: Simon & Schuster, 1992); Thomas Sowell, *Inside American Education* (New York: The Free Press, 1993).

10. "Return of the Storm Troopers" (editorial), *Wall Street Journal,* April 10, 1991, p. A22.

11. David Beers, "PC? B.S." *Mother Jones,* September/October 1991, p. 64.

12. Ken Fireman, "'Political Correctness' in Dispute," *Newsday,* May 12, 1991, p. 34.

13. Katherine M. Skiba, "Women Underrepresented at UW in Leadership Roles, Study Shows," *Milwaukee Journal,* June 23, 1994, pp. B1, B5.

14. *Digest of Education Statistics, 29th ed.* (Washington, D.C.: U.S. Government Printing Office, 1993), p. 232.

15. Russell Chandler, "Father Curran Suspended from Catholic University," *Los Angeles Times,* January 13, 1987, p. 1.

16. In UCLA's College of Engineering and Applied Sciences, there is the Rockwell International Chair of Engineering, the Northrop Chair in Electrical Engineering, the TRW Chair in Electrical Engineering, the

Hughes Aircraft Company Chair in Manufacturing Engineering, and the Nippon Sheet Glass Company Chair in Materials Science. UCLA also houses the John E. Anderson School of Business, named for the tycoon who gave it $15 million in 1987, and the Olin Center for Policy, an on-campus advocacy center that is funded by a million-dollar grant from the John M. Olin Foundation.

17. Julie L. Nicklin, "Philip Morris Boosts Aid to Colleges, but Critics Question Tobacco Company's Motives," *Chronicle of Higher Education*, October 13, 1993, pp. A37, A39.

18. Telephone interview of February 12, 1992.

19. "Across the USA," *USA Today*, March 9, 1993, p. 8A; Goldie Blumenstyk, "Philanthropic Notes," *Chronicle of Higher Education*, March 17, 1993, p. A36; "Philanthropy Notes," *Chronicle of Higher Education*, May 12, 1993, p. A35. According to these reports, Janet MacDonald, the deputy treasurer of the University and Community College System of Nevada, said that the regents initially rejected the ACE "gift" because a company cannot contract for "research and count it as a charitable donation." Two months later, after University of Nevada at Las Vegas officials renegotiated the agreement with ACE Denken, the board of regents approved the "gift." The new agreement still called for the university to hold an annual seminar on gambling, but it did not allow ACE management to choose the topic or determine the invitation list. However, the new agreement did not prohibit ACE from suggesting topics for the seminar or a list of people who should be invited. The agreement still called for the university to publish a journal, albeit with fewer restrictions than called for in the original agreement. Finally, the new agreement called for ACE and the university to review their collaboration every five years, rather than having the agreement last indefinitely. The board of regents approved the new agreement, stating that it was now without strings. "The ambiguities are gone," Janet MacDonald said of the new agreement.

20. "Give & Take," *Chronicle of Higher Education*, November 25, 1992, p. A21; "$100 Million Donated to New Jersey College," *Washington Times*, July 7, 1992, p. A5.

21. "School Aid on One Condition," *Philadelphia Inquirer*, November 13, 1992, p. A1; "NJ Legislators and Unions Assail Henry Rowan's Scholarship Rule," *Philadelphia Inquirer*, November 14, 1992, p. A1.

22. For example, this classification, first employed by the Carnegie Foundation, is used in "Pay and Benefits of Leaders at 190 Private Colleges and Universities," *Chronicle of Higher Education*, May 5, 1993, pp. A17-A24.

23. L. Stuart Ditzen, "Colleges Learn Price of Patents," *Orlando Sentinel Tribune*, May 6, 1990, p. D1.

24. University of Minnesota president Nils Hasselmo typifies the attitude of university administrators. Although student satisfaction at his university was rated 122nd among major universities in a *U.S. News & World*

Report survey, Hasselmo lauded his university's accomplishments in a *Star Tribune* commentary, writing that "we have become one of the nation's leading universities in patents secured." See Nils Hasselmo, "'U' Ties to Industry Result in Private, Public Benefits," *Minneapolis Star Tribune,* June 7, 1992, p. 25A.

25. *Ibid.*

26. Linda Williams, "Academia Wises Up on Patents," *Los Angeles Times,* March 16, 1990, p. A1.

27. Felicity Barringer, "Drug Patent Debate Turns on Risks, Costs," *Washington Post,* May 13, 1983, p. A17; "Bristol-Myers' License for Anticancer Drug is Extended," PR Newswire, January 15, 1988.

28. Ernest Hollings, "The Ruins of Reaganism," *Washington Post,* April 30, 1989, p. C2.

29. Eric Schmitt, "House Battle Threatens Big Research Universities with Loss of Millions," *New York Times,* August 17, 1994, p. A9.

30. Jim Glassman, "University Research: Private Investment and Public Interests," *At the Crossroads* (Northern Tier Land Grant Accountability Project), July 1993, pp. 1-2, 7.

31. William Honan, "Cost of 4-year Degree Passes $100,000 Mark," *New York Times,* May 4, 1994, p. A13.

32. *The World Almanac and Book of Facts 1994* (Mahwah, NJ: Funk & Wagnals, 1993), p. 200.

33. "Financial Aid: Attempts at Diversity Create Bidding Wars," *Daily Political Report* (American Political Network), October 7, 1992; Rhonda Reynolds, "Doctorates Up...But to What Degree?," *Black Enterprise,* June 1994, p. 40.

34. Peter H. Stone, "Business Widens Role in Conservative 'War of Ideas,'" *Washington Post,* May 12, 1985, p. F1. Smith-Kline Beckman became part of the Beecham Group PLC in 1989.

35. Philip Stevens, "Universities Find a New Partner," *World Press Review,* October 1986, p. 37; Anthony DePalma, "Universities' Reliance on Companies Raises Vexing Questions on Research," *New York Times,* March 17, 1993, p. B9.

36. Committee on Government Operations, House of Representatives, 101st Congress (2nd session), *Is Science for Sale?* (Washington, D.C.: Government Printing Office, 1989), p. 134.

37. Philip Stevens, *World Press Review, op. cit.*

38. "Center for Technology Venturing" (brochure), Bureau of Business Research, University of Texas at Austin; IC^2 Institute, *Annual Report 1989-90* (Austin: The University of Texas, 1990), pp. 5-7.

39. E. A. Torriero, "Biosphere 2: Futurist Study or Stunt?" *Ottawa Citizen,* September 26, 1991, p. G.

40. Joel Achenbach, "Biosphere 2: Bogus New World?" *Washington Post,* January 8, 1992, p. C1; Marc Cooper, "Take This Terrarium and Shove It," *Village Voice,* April 2, 1992, p. 31. *Village Voice* reporter Marc

Cooper described the venture as a space cult, headed by a former theater troupe and commune leader, who once called himself "Johnny Dolphin." Rocky Stewart, a computer programmer who worked at the Bisophere but quit the project because of the scientific chicanery, describes Biosphere 2 as an aboveground "submarine with plants in it." The scientific credentials of Johnny Dolphin and others involved with the Biosphere are also a sham. Their credentials are from the London-based Institute of Ecotechnics, which Dolphin and Bass established. A documentary made by the Canadian Broadcasting Company discovered that the institute, which granted "degrees" to six officials of the Biosphere, was little more than a London cafe and art gallery.

41. Nick Ravo, "Bass Family Gives Yale $20 Million for Ecology Institute," *New York Times,* May 8, 1990, p. B1.

42. "Current Mission to End on September 17, 1994," press release from Space Biosphere Ventures public affairs director Chris Helms, dated August 16, 1994; Victor Dricks, "Science in Whose Interest?" *Phoenix Gazette,* March 16, 1992, pp. A1, A6.

43. "The Dream, the Reality, the Program," promotional materials from Karl Eller Center (1991).

44. The Alliance includes such organizations as the Children's Defense Fund, the National Education Association, and the Consumer's Union.

45. Alliance for Justice, *Justice for Sale* (Washington, D.C.: Alliance for Justice, 1993), pp. 33-34, 75-79.

Notes to Chapter Two

1. "Boren Denies Plan to Quit," *Sacramento Bee*, April 2, 1994, p. A14.

2. "Boren to Become OU President," United Press International, April 27, 1994 (BC Cycle).

3. A study by the Center for Responsive Politics, a nonpartisan research group, found that in some industries, particularly those where Boren got his contributions, CEOs contributed more to political candidates than did their PACs. For a discussion, see Keith White, "Boren, Synar Forgo PAC Money, Get Lots from Special Interests," Gannett News Service, June 30, 1992.

4. Keith White, "Boren Widens Money Lead over Republican Challenger," Gannett News Service, October 22, 1990.

5. Ray Tuttle, "Energy to Lose Ally: Domestic Industry Not Looking forward to Boren's Departure from Congress," *Tulsa World,* April 28, 1994, p. B1.

6. *Who's Who in America 1992-1993, 47th ed.* (New Providence, NJ: Marquis Who's Who, 1992), pp. 1811, 2992.

7. "Michigan State Picks a Banker as President," *New York Times,* August 19, 1993, p. A8.

8. Ben H. Bagdikian, *The Media Monopoly* (Boston: Beacon Press, 1987), p. 51.

9. *Who's Who in America 1992-1993, op. cit.,* p. 3100. *Religion Within the Limits of Reason Alone* was translated by Theodore Greene and Hoyt Hudson.

10. For the number of times that Silber's academic works were cited by other scholars, see the *Social Science Citation Index 1956-1965, 10 Year Cumulation* (Philadelphia: Institute for Scientific Information, 1989), col. 18711; and *Social Science Citation Index 1966-1970, Five Year Cumulation* (Philadelphia: Institute for Scientific Information, 1989), col. 24203.

11. Fox Butterfield, "President of Boston University Finds He Is Entangled in His Own Success," *New York Times,* February 9, 1993, p. A8.

12. American Council on Education, *American Colleges and Universities, 12th ed.* (New York: Walter de Gruyter, 1983), p. 844; American Council on Education, *American Colleges and Universities, 14th ed.* (New York: Walter de Gruyter, 1992), p. 768.

13. Eloise Salholz, "J-School for Afghan Rebels," *Newsweek,* March 30, 1987, p. 75.

14. Wendell Jamieson, "Afghan Reporter Project Nears End, But Divisions at BU Might Linger," *Boston Globe,* December 27, 1987, p. 36.

15. Jerrold H. Footlick, "Eleven Exemplary Journalism Schools," *Gannett Center Journal,* Summer 1988, pp. 68-76. BU didn't even get an honorable mention in Footlick's article. John C. Schweitzer, "Research Article Productivity by Mass Communication Scholars," *Journalism Quarterly,* Summer 1988, pp. 479-484, did not list BU among the leading mass communication research universities. Schweitzer's rankings were based on research productivity.

16. "Holdings of Research Libraries," *Chronicle of Higher Education,* March 10, 1993, p. A8.

17. Charles Claffey, "Separating Myth from Maitre," *Boston Globe,* July 12, 1991, p. 41.

18. Courtney Leatherman, "New Eruption at Boston U.," *Chronicle of Higher Education,* December 8, 1993, p. A27.

19. "Endowed Positions at Boston University," Development Office, Boston University (undated).

20. Thomas Toch and Ted Slafsky, "The Scientific Pork Barrel," *U.S. News & World Report,* March 1, 1993, pp. 58-59; Congressional Research Service, *The Distribution of Apparent Academic Earmarks in the Federal Government's FY 1992 Appropriations Bills* (Washington, D.C.: House Committee on Science, Space and Technology, September 1992).

21. "Overhead-Cost Rate Declines at Major Research Universities," *Chronicle of Higher Education,* December 8, 1993, p. A34.

22. Goldie Blumenstyk, "Boston U.'s President and Trustees Face Questions about Business Practices and Conflicts of Interest," *Chronicle of Higher Education,* February 10, 1993, pp. A27-A28; "Boston U. Agrees to New Policies on Top Officers," *New York Times,* December 17, 1993, p. A15.

23. Douglas Lederman, "Survey Reveals Salaries of Executives and Highest-Paid Staff Members at 190 Colleges," *Chronicle of Higher Education,* May 5, 1993, pp. A13-A15.

24. Douglas Lederman and Denise Magner, "What College Leaders Earn," *Chronicle of Higher Education,* September 14, 1994, pp. A25-A27.

25. Anthony Flint and Stephen Kurkjian, "BU Board Is Bucking Accountability Trend," *Boston Globe,* January 28, 1993, p. 17; Goldie Blumenstyk, *op. cit.*

26. Susan Chira, "Head of Boston U. Says He Didn't Lie," *New York Times,* March 17, 1993, p. B9.

27. Courtney Leatherman, *op. cit.*, p. A16.

28. *American Colleges and Universities, 14th ed.* (New York: Walter de Gruyter, 1993), p. 920; *American Colleges and Universities, 12th ed.* (New York: Walter de Gruyter, 1983), p. 1014.

29. William Honan, "Columbia Installs Its 18th President," *New York Times,* October 5, 1993, p. A14.

30. For discussion of university endowments and their earnings, see Julie Nicklin, "Colleges' Earnings on Endowment Averaged 13.1% in Fiscal 1992," *Chronicle of Higher Education,* February 10, 1993, pp. A29-A31.

31. William Honan, "Woman Is Penn President; The First in the Ivy League," *New York Times,* December 7, 1993, p. A8.

32. Anthony Flint, "Michigan State Head Will Be Tufts President," *Boston Globe,* May 20, 1992, p. 1.

33. Douglas Lederman, *op. cit.*

34. "Presidents Under Fire for High Pay and Perks," *Milwaukee Journal,* March 28, 1993, p. 14.

35. "The Peripatetic Chancellor," *New York Times,* March 1, 1994, p. A14.

36. Maria Newman, "CUNY Chancellor's Time Spent with Corporate Boards Is at Issue," *New York Times,* February 22, 1994, pp. 1, 8.

37. Douglas Lederman, *op. cit.*, p. A14.

38. *Ibid.*, p. A13.

39. Tyler L. Chin and Dennis Chapman, "Rose Bowl Proceeds Will Pay for VIPs' Trips," *Milwaukee Journal,* December 19, 1993, p. B5.

40. Ray Gibson, "University's Perks Face Examination," *Chicago Tribune,* May 15, 1986, p. 1C.

41. Thomas Heath, "GMU's Chief's Sweet Deal on Va. Tract Reflects Hazel's Ties to University," *Washington Post,* February 22, 1990, p. D4.

42. "Business Leaders Gear Up to Oust Moore in Fairfax Race," United Press International, August 19, 1991 (BC cycle).

43. "State Notes," *Chronicle of Higher Education,* May 5, 1993, p. A33.

44. "Subcommittee Expands Inquiry to All Universities," United Press International, Illinois Region, May 21, 1986; Ray Gibson and Jerry Huston, "Audit Finds NIU Waste, Misspending," *Chicago Tribune,* April 23, 1987, p. 1C.

45. "U. of Minnesota Head Resigns," *Chicago Tribune*, March 15, 1988, p. 3.

46. Courtney Leatherman, "Severance Package for University Chancellor," *Chronicle of Higher Education,* August 14, 1991, p. A13.

47. Tom Philp and Lisa Lapin, "Outgoing UC President Chided Gave Extra Year's Pay to Retiring Executive," *Sacramento Bee,* May 13, 1993, p. A1.

48. Peter Passell, "One Top College Price Tag: Why So Low, and So High?" *New York Times,* July 27, 1994, pp. A1, B8.

49. Karen Grassmuck, "Throughout the 80s, Colleges Hired More Non-Teaching Staff than Other Employees," *Chronicle of Higher Education,* August 14, 1991, p. A22.

50. Dorin Schumacher, *Get Funded!* (Newbury Park, CA: Sage Publications, 1992), pp. 229, 252.

51. Richard E. Lapchick and John B. Slaughter, *The Rules of the Game* (New York: Macmillan Publishing, 1989), p. 12.

52. *Ibid.*, p. 137.

53. Murray Sperber, *College Sports, Inc.* (New York: Henry Holt and Company, 1990), pp. 149-150.

54. *Hoover Institution Report 1990* (Stanford, CA: Stanford University, 1991), p. 32.

55. Martin Anderson, "The Galls of Ivy: Our Professors Do Everything But Teach," *Washington Post,* October 18, 1992, p. C3.

56. O. Casey Corr, "School Ties—University of Washington Turns Laboratory Discoveries into Business Alliances," *Seattle Times,* May 16, 1994, p. E1.

57. Linda Williams, "Academia Wises Up on Patents," *Los Angeles Times,* March 16, 1990, p. A1; O. Casey Corr, "School Ties—University of Washington Turns Laboratory Discoveries into Business Alliances," *ibid*; L. Stuart Ditzen, "Colleges Learn Price of Patents," *Orlando Sentinel Tribune,* May 6, 1990, p. D1.

58. Hearing before the Select Committee on Children, Youths and Families, 102nd Congress (2nd session), *College Education: Paying More and Getting Less* (Washington, D.C.: U.S. Government Printing Office, 1993).

59. *Digest of Education Statistics* (Washington, D.C.: National Center for Education Statistics, 1993), pp. 201, 227. The enrollment growth was calculated on full-time equivalent enrollments. When total enrollment is used, the growth in student enrollment was 11.9 percent.

60. Hearing before the Select Subcommittee on Children, Youths and Family, *op. cit.*, p. 4; Karen Glassmuck, "Throughout the 80s, Colleges Hired More Non-Teaching Staff than Other Employees," *op. cit.;* William Honan, "Cost of 4-year Degree Passes $100,000 Mark," *New York Times*, May 14, 1994, p. A13; Bob Dart, "Americans Pay More, Get Less From College," *Atlanta Journal and Constitution*, September 15, 1992, p. A7.

61. "AAUP Survey Finds Faculty Salaries Rose 2.4% in 1992-93," *Chronicle of Higher Education*, April 14, 1993, p. A19.

Notes to Chapter Three

1. "Retarded Boys Fed Radioactive Milk in Experiment in 1950s," *Milwaukee Journal*, December 27, 1991, p. A7; Scott Allen, "MIT Records Show Wider Radioactive Testing at Fernald," *Boston Globe*, December 31, 1993, p. 1; Keith Schneider, "Nuclear Scientists Irradiated People in Secret Research," *New York Times*, December 17, 1993, pp. A1, A14.

2. "Doubt Was Cast in 1966 on Radiation Experiment," *New York Times*, March 3, 1994, p. A7.

3. Stephen Budiansky, Erica Goode, and Ted Gest, "The Cold War Experiments," *U.S. News & World Report*, January 24, 1994, pp. 36-37. The United States financed a host of other ethically questionable studies. For example, during the 1970s, University of Washington medical researchers exposed the testicles of 100 healthy prisoners to high levels of radiation from X-ray machines to determine for the government the levels that created sterility. The inmates were never fully informed of the cancer dangers associated with participation in the experiments. Columbia University medical researchers injected radioactive materials into patients to determine the rate at which radioactivity was absorbed into tissues. See Keith Schneider, "Nuclear Scientists Irradiated People in Secret Research," *op. cit.*

4. "A New Research Support Facility," *Research Profile* (UWM), Vol. 16 (3), pp. 31-32; "UWM Contract Research/Technical Consulting," Office of Industrial Research and Technology Transfer (UWM), undated.

5. Tony Caridea, "Hasselmo Admits Need for Better Damage Control, But Insists He Has the Helm," *Minneapolis Star Tribune*, February 18, 1993.

6. Susan Diesenhouse, "Harvard's New Test-tube Business," *New York Times*, August 22, 1993, p. C4.

7. "Scripps Imposes Limits on Sandoz Deal," *Marketletter*, July 19, 1993.

8. The congressional investigations were launched because Scripps received more than $69 million of U.S. government funding during 1992.

9. "Scripps Reworking Sandoz Contract," *Minneapolis Star Tribune*, July 7, 1993, p. 3D; Craig Rose, "New Scripps-Sandoz Accord Proposed," *San Diego Union-Tribune*, February 25, 1994, p. C1.

10. Daniel Golden, "Dana-Farber Pact with Corporation Questioned," *Boston Globe,* December 4, 1993, p. 1.

11. Julie Nicklin, "University Deals with Drug Companies Raise Concern over Autonomy, Secrecy," *Chronicle of Higher Education,* March 24, 1993, pp. A25-A26; Kenneth M. Ludmerer, *Learning to Heal* (New York: Basic Books, 1985), p. 274.

12. Goldie Blumenstyk, "Business and Philanthropy," *Chronicle of Higher Education,* March 31, 1993, p. A26.

13. Until the government put a stop to it, administrators at the Scripps Research Institute received stocks in corporations that received licenses from Scripps. The stocks were given by the research institute, not the corporations. Scientists at Scripps received "stock compensation directly from the companies," reports Chris Kraul, "Scripps Research to End Stock Awards," *Los Angeles Times,* December 22, 1993, p. 3D.

14. Maura Lerner, "Despite Rules, 'U' Reluctant to Prevent Conflicts of Interest," *Minneapolis Star Tribune,* May 31, 1992, p. 8A.

15. Peter G. Gosselin, "Flawed Study Helps Doctors Profit on Drugs," *Boston Globe,* October 19, 1988, pp. 1, 16-17.

16. U.S. House of Representatives, Committee on Government Operations, *Are Scientific Misconduct and Conflicts of Interest Hazardous to Our Health?* House Report 101-688, September 10, 1990 (Washington, D.C.: U.S. Government Printing Office, 1990), pp. 19-27.

17. Eliot Marshall, "When Commerce and Academe Collide," *Science,* April 13, 1990, p. 152.

18. Robert Bazell, "Virus, Science and Society—Biomedical Scientists, Universities and Commercial Conflicts of Interest," *New Republic,* November 9, 1992, p. 21.

19. "Pay and Benefits of Leaders at 190 Private Colleges and Universities: A Survey," *Chronicle of Higher Education,* May 5, 1993, p. A18.

20. William C. Smith, Jr., *Report on Medical School Faculty Salaries 1991-1992* (Washington, D.C.: Association of Medical Colleges, March 1992), p. 12.

21. Paul Bernstein, "What's Your Ph.D. Ratio?" *Forbes,* August 15, 1983, p. 112; Peter Hall, "Advances in a Special Sector; The Business of Biotechnology," *Financial World,* April 3, 1984, p. 8.

22. "Human Monoclonal Antibody Therapy Shows Promise in Clinical Trials," Business Wire, February 13, 1991.

23. Elizabeth J. Ziegler, *et al.*, "Treatment of Gram-Negative Bacteremia and Septic Shock with HA-1A Human Monoclonal Antibody Against Endotoxin," *New England Journal of Medicine,* February 14, 1991, pp. 429-436.

24. Peter Hall, "Advances in a Special Sector; The Business of Biotechnology," *op. cit.*, p. 8: Paul Bernstein, "What's Your Ph.D. Ratio?" *op. cit.*, p. 112.

25. Gina Kolata, "Halted at the Market Door: How a $1 Billion Drug Failed," *New York Times,* February 12, 1993, pp. A1, A9.

26. Colleen Cordes, "Research Project on Ear Infections Dramatizes Challenge of Conflicts," *Chronicle of Higher Education,* March 3, 1993, pp. A23, A28.

27. House Committee on Government Operations, *op. cit.,* pp. 28-34.

28. *Ibid.*

29. Maura Lerner, "Professor Sues 'U,' Claiming Harassment for Whistleblowing," *Minneapolis Star Tribune,* November 14, 1992, p. 1B. The university spends millions of dollars investigating and defending itself, according to Jenifer Waters, "Huge Legal Bill for U of M," *Minneapolis-St. Paul CityBusiness,* October 15, 1993, p. 1. The university spent nearly $4 million for lawyers in just one case.

30. Debra Blum, "Scandals at U. of Minnesota Prompt Outside Review of Medical School," *Chronicle of Higher Education,* April 7, 1993, p. A18; Joe Rigert, "Hasselmo Says 'U' Acted Properly in Research Probes," *Minneapolis Star Tribune,* September 1, 1992, p. 1B; Nancy Livingston, "FBI, IRS Agents Raid Najarian's Office at U," *St. Paul Pioneer Press,* October 6, 1993, p. 3B; "IRS, FBI Raid Offices of Najarian, Group at 'U'," *Minneapolis Star Tribune,* October 6, 1993, p. 1A.

31. Laura Baenen, "Medical School's Woes Linked to Ethics," *Los Angeles Times,* June 13, 1993, p. 17A; "IRS, FBI Raid Offices of Najarian, Group at 'U'," *ibid.,* p. 1A.

32. Maura Lerner and Joe Rigert, "Whistleblowers Are Anything But Welcome at the 'U'," *Minneapolis Star Tribune,* December 31, 1992, p. 14A.

33. Joe Rigert, "Hasselmo Says 'U' Acted Properly in Research Probes," *Minneapolis Star Tribune,* September 1, 1992, p. 1B.

34. Doug Grow, "Jury Gives to Garfinkel's Former Aide What 'U' Didn't—Vindication," *Minneapolis Star Tribune,* August 8, 1993, p. 3B; Patrick Sweeney, "Renowned U Professor Found Guilty in Fraud Case," *St. Paul Pioneer Press,* August 6, 1993, pp. 1C, 4C; Maura Lerner, "Jury Convicts Garfinkel of 5 Fraud Counts," *Minneapolis Star Tribune,* August 8, 1993, pp. 1A, 10A; Joe Rigert, "Top Child Psychiatrist at 'U' Indicted on Charges of Fraud," *Minneapolis Star Tribune,* February 17, 1993, pp. 1A, 11A.

35. House Committee on Government Operations, *op. cit.,* pp. 11-12.

36. Diana Zuckerman, "Why Has the NIH Done Nothing to Minimize Conflicts of Interest in Science?" *Chronicle of Higher Education,* October 13, 1993, p. B2.

37. Joseph Palca, "NIH Conflict-of-Interest Guidelines Shot Down," *Science,* January 1990, p. 154.

38. "Some of the Voices from the Chorus of Protest," *Science,* January 1990, p. 155.

39. Eliot Marshall, "Harvard's Tough New Rules," *Science,* April 1990, p. 155.

40. "Instructions for Authors," *Journal of the American Medical Association*, January 1, 1992, p. 41. A less rigorous wording of the disclosure requirement can be found in "Instructions for Authors," *Journal of the American Medical Association*, January 13, 1989, p. 217.

41. Jenny Scott, "Researcher to Clarify Ties to Drug Company," *Los Angeles Times*, March 24, 1990, p. 3B.

42. William Broad and Nicholas Wade, *Betrayers of the Truth* (New York: Simon and Schuster, 1982).

43. At the University of Minnesota, each medical department, such as hematology and gastroenterology, operates private medical practices that work out of university facilities. These practices are independent corporations, despite their links to the state university. The corporations make their money by charging patients for medical services that are provided at the university's hospital and clinic, even though the services are frequently performed on university time. The department heads usually run the private practices; some are legally owned by the department heads. Others are structured as nonprofit corporations. These corporations pay their professors directly, so no one except the department head, the professor, and the university's "private practice monitor" know what their salaries are. Not even the university president and board of regents know. They only know what the professors are being paid by the university, and this is frequently far less than the amount paid by the corporation. For a discussion of the corruption associated with these operations, see Maura Lerner, Joe Rigert, and Nikhil Deogun, "'U' Urology Chief Capitalizes on a System that is Open to Abuse," *Minneapolis Star Tribune*, April 4, 1993, pp. 1A, 20A.

Notes to Chapter Four

1. "Russ Haley & Associates," in Janice McLean (ed.), *1987-1988 Consultants and Consulting Organizations Directory* (Detroit: Gale Research Co., 1986); Russell Haley, "Benefit Segments: Backwards and Forwards," *Journal of Advertising Research*, February/March 1984, p. 20.

2. Thomas J. Reynolds and Charles Gengler, "A Strategic Framework for Assessing Advertising: The Animatic vs. Finished Issue," *Journal of Advertising Research*, October/November 1991, p. 61.

3. Marilyn Yaquinto, "Competitiveness: Consultant to Deliver Advice on Overhauling Postal Service," *Los Angeles Times*, July 22, 1992, p. A5; *Consultants and Consulting Organizations Directory*, 13th ed. (Detroit: Gale Research Co., 1993), p. 1426.

4. "A Database That Lets You Browse for an Expert," *Business Week*, July 1, 1991, p. 79; "Easy Access to University Research Capabilities," *Inside R&D*, July 10, 1991, p. 8.

5. The jury in the Cipollone case was the first to decide in favor of a plaintiff in a civil suit against a tobacco company, ordering Liggett to pay damages of $400,000 to Antonio Cipollone. The jury found that Liggett was

partially to blame for Rose Cipollone's death. See Morton Mintz, "Jury Finds Tobacco Shares Blame in Death," *Washington Post,* June 13, 1988, p. A1.

6. The testimony was obtained from Morton Mintz, "Judge Questions a Tobacco Company Witness," *Washington Post,* April 16, 1988, p. D12; Donald Janson, "Jury Hears Testimony on Impact of Cigarette Ads," *New York Times,* April 17, 1988, p. 44; and Frances Ann Burns, "Expert in Tobacco Trial Says Ads Don't Work," United Press International (BC Cycle), April 13, 1988.

7. See Richard Pollay, "Pertinent Research and Impertinent Opinions," *Journal of Advertising,* December 1993, pp. 110-117.

8. Claude R. Martin, "Ethical Advertising Research Standards: Three Case Studies," *Journal of Advertising,* September 1994, pp. 17-29.

9. Scott Ward, "The Effects of Tobacco Advertising on Adolescent Smoking Initiation and Smoking Maintenance: Overview of a Group Seminar," *International Journal of Advertising* (Special Report), Spring 1990, p. 88; Lawrence Soley, "Smoke-Filled Rooms and Research," *Journal of Advertising,* December 1993, pp. 108-110.

10. "Statement of Scott Ward," Hearings before the Subcommittee on Health and the Environment, 99th Congress (2nd session), *Advertising of Tobacco Products,* Serial 99-167 (Washington, D.C.: U.S. Government Printing Office, 1987), p. 666.

11. Larry King and Bill Frischling, "Wharton Professor Arrested on Sex Charges," *Philadelphia Inquirer,* October 5, 1993, p. B1; Larry King, "New Sex Charges Against Professor," *Philadelphia Inquirer,* October 9, 1993, p. B1.

12. Janice Perrone, "Tobacco Firms Attack JAMA Ad Studies," *American Medical News,* March 2, 1992, p. 3.

13. Richard Mizerski, Brenda Sonner, and Katherine Straughn, "A Re-Evaluation of the Reported Influence of the Joe Camel Trade Character on Cigarette Trial and Use by Minors," in *Proceedings of the 1993 Conference of the American Academy of Advertising* (Columbia, MO: The University of Missouri, 1993), p. 1.

14. "Statement of Roger Blackwell," Subcommittee on Health and the Environment, 99th Congress (2nd session), *Advertising of Tobacco Products,* Serial 99-167 (Washington, D.C.: U.S. Government Printing Office, 1987).

15. Nathan Cobb, "Consulting the Stars," *Boston Globe,* November 10, 1991, p. 14.

16. Carol Boyer and Darrell Lewis, *And on the Seventh Day: Faculty Consulting and Supplemental Income* (Washington, D.C.: Association for the Study of Higher Education, 1985).

17. Hearing Before the Select Committee on Children, Youth and Families, 102nd Congress (2nd session), *College Education: Paying More*

and Getting Less (Washington, D.C.: U.S. Government Printing Office, 1993).

18. Michigan State University, *Budgetary Information and Salary Schedules 1993-1994* (East Lansing, MI: Michigan State University, 1993), pp.167-194.

19. The University of Wisconsin, *1993-1994 Budget,* Vol. II (UW-Madison) (Madison: University of Wisconsin, 1993), pp. 100-102, 232, 244, 246-247.

20. Barbara Rehm, "Washington Briefing an Insider's Guide to Capital Issues," *American Banker,* April 24, 1989, p. 6.

21. *Ibid.*

22. Telephone interview of December 1, 1992.

23. "Tobacco Institute Testifies that Tobacco Advertising Bill Would Not Reduce Youth Smoking," Business Wire, July 25, 1989.

24. Scott Ward, "A Ban on Tobacco Advertising Would be Ineffective," *Quill,* December 1986, p.29; telephone interview with former *Quill* editor Mike Moore.

25. Edward S. Herman, "The Institutionalization of Bias in Economics," *Media, Culture and Society* 4 (1982), p. 282.

26. Ernest Holsendolph, "Bell's Fees to Experts Cited by Rivals," *New York Times,* June 8, 1982, p. D1.

27. *Ibid.*

28. Jagdish N. Sheth, "Caller ID Benefits Outweigh Perils," *Chicago Tribune,* April 20, 1991, p. 17.

29. "Voice of the People" (Letter), *Chicago Tribune,* May 16, 1991, p. 26. According to Sheth, conflicts of interest arise only when "one expresses his or her viewpoint contrary to one's belief." Since he believes in caller ID, no conflict of interest exists for him, Sheth contends.

30. See March 1988, December 1989, and September 1990 issues of *Journal of Consumer Research.*

31. Charles Sykes, *Profscam* (New York: St. Martin's Press, 1988), p. 110.

32. Lyman W. Porter and Lawrence E. McKibbin, *Management Education and Development* (New York: McGraw-Hill, 1988), pp. 173, 180.

33. Lawrence Soley, "The High Price of Wisdom," *Minneapolis City Pages,* July 3, 1991, p. 6.

34. Lawrence Soley, "Nobody's Business But Theirs," *Minneapolis City Pages,* July 10, 1991, p. 6.

35. *Ibid.*

36. "A Long Shot, at Best," *U.S. News & World Report,* March 21, 1994, pp. 72-73.

37. Risa Berg, "UW Buildings Are Study in Contrasts," *Milwaukee Journal,* October 24, 1993, p. B5.

38. "Financier Contributes $20 Million to Michigan State Business Schools," *Minneapolis Star Tribune,* June 26, 1991, p. 1D.

39. "Naming Opportunities," *Transacta, the MSU Business Alumni Magazine,* Spring 1993, pp. 2-4.

40. "Flap Surrounds MSU Business Dean Search," United Press International (BC Cycle), February 2, 1994.

41. *New York University Bulletin, Graduate Division 1991-1993* (New York: New York University, 1991), p. 10.

42. Other business schools named for tycoons include those at the University of Minnesota (named for Curtis Carlson), Cornell University (named for Samuel Curtis Johnson), Brigham Young University (named for J. Willard and Alice S. Marriott), the University of California at Berkeley (named for Walter A. Haas), the University of Pittsburgh (named for Joseph M. Katz), and Duke University (named for J. B. Fuqua).

43. *The Focal Point,* January 1993 (Madison, WI: A.C. Nielsen Center for Marketing Research, 1993), p. 7.

44. "The New Face of Marketing Research—Focusing on Tomorrow's Trends" (Madison, WI: A.C. Nielsen Center for Marketing Research, undated).

45. *A.C. Nielsen Center for Marketing Research* (Madison, WI: University of Wisconsin, undated), p. 8.

46. *Ibid.,* p. 6.

47. *Spring 1994 Timetable* (Madison, WI: University of Wisconsin-Madison, 1994), p. 35; *Fall 1994-1995 Timetable* (Madison, WI: University of Wisconsin, 1994), p. 35; *1993-1994 Budget,* Vol. II (Madison, WI: University of Wisconsin, 1993), p. 102.

48. Telephone interview of June 7, 1994.

49. Telephone interview of June 27, 1994.

50. Colman McCarthy, "Academia's Stoop Laborers," *Washington Post,* September 28, 1991, p. A27.

51. The salary information was provided by Office of Academic Affairs, Murphy Hall 3109, UCLA. Based on UCLA's *Schedule of Classes* for the Fall 1993, Winter 1994, and Spring 1994 quarters.

52. Telephone interview of June 27, 1994.

53. Bill Vlasic, "Industrialist Aims Grant at Emerging Economies," *Detroit News,* April 24, 1992, p. E1.

54. "New Tie With Cathay-Pacific," *Michigan Today,* December 1993, p. 4; Barry Porter, "Cathay Business School Plan Gets Airborne," *South China Morning Post,* October 8, 1993, p. 3.

55. Lori Bongiorno, "B-Schools Bitten by the Global Bug," *Business Week,* October 25, 1993, p. 106.

Notes to Chapter Five

1. Richard Harris Smith, *OSS* (Berkeley: University of California Press, 1981), p. 13.

2. Christopher Simpson, in *Science of Coercion* (New York: Oxford University Press, 1994), describes the close relationship between the U.S. State Department and prominent university psychologists, sociologists, and political scientists during the postwar era. Simpson calls these social scientists "university entrepreneurs," and shows that the majority of dollars going to Paul Lazarsfeld's Bureau of Applied Social Research at Columbia University, Hadley Cantril's Institute for International Social Research at Princeton, and Ithiel de Sola Pool's Center for International Studies at MIT came from the U.S. government, which bankrolled research concerned with propaganda, persuasion, and "psychological warfare."

3. Christopher Simpson, *ibid.*, pp. 4, 69.

4. Pressures included the fear of being named a "communist" or "fellow-traveller" by members of the House Un-American Activities Committee, Senator Joseph McCarthy, or their ilk, as occurred with Johns Hopkins University professor Owen J. Lattimore.

5. The averages for social science professors were calculated from table reported in Denise Magner, "Academic Fields Where Women Predominate Pay Least, Survey Finds," *Chronicle of Higher Education*, June 22, 1994, p. A16. The medical salaries are from William C. Smith, Jr., *Report on Medical School Faculty Salaries 1991-1992* (Washington, D.C.: Association of Medical Colleges, March 1992), p. 12. Many medical specializations pay more than anesthesiology. The average salary of assistant professors of thoracic and cardiovascular surgery was $247,800 in 1991.

6. Sue DeWine, *The Consultant's Craft* (New York: St. Martin's Press, 1994), p. 361.

7. "Competitive Papers: Applied Research," Conference of the American Academy of Advertising, April 9, 1994, Salon D.

8. *Ibid.*

9. Joan Vennochi, "What They Don't Teach You at Harvard Business School," *Working Woman,* February 1993, p. 51.

10. Throughout Kanter's tenure as editor of the *Review*, she continued to do consulting, which reportedly interfered with her ability to oversee the publication. The staff became resentful of her absentee management style, and several assistant editors resigned. As a result of the discord—Harvard's public relations office claims there wasn't any discord—Kanter resigned as editor, but became a vice chair of the newly created Harvard Business School Publishing Group, which oversees the *Review* and other income-producing ventures, such as instructional videotapes. One of the videotapes that the venture distributes is a set of tapes of Kanter discussing her innovative management techniques, which sells for $2,000. See Alison Leigh Cowan, "Management Citadel Rocked by Unruliness," *New York Times,* September 26, 1991, p. D1; Paul Hemp, "Shake-up at the Harvard Business Review," *The Boston Globe,* June 2, 1992, p. 37.

The Review has repeatedly been accused of killing stories that might upset Harvard donors, such as IBM and Japanese corporations. See John

Markoff, "Harvard Business Review Cancels IBM Article," *New York Times*, December 21, 1992, p. C3; Adam Smith, "Japan Inc. Is Still in Business," *New York Times Book Review*, March 19, 1995, p. 7.

11. Jacob Jacoby, "Interpersonal Perceptual Accuracy as a Function of Dogmatism," *Journal of Experimental Social Psychology* 7 (1971), pp. 221-236; Jacob Jacoby, "Time Perspective and Dogmatism: A Replication," *Journal of Social Psychology* 79 (1969), pp. 281-282; Jacob Jacoby, "Birth Rank and Pre-experimental Anxiety," *Journal of Social Psychology* 76 (1968), pp. 9-11; Jacob Jacoby, "Open-mindedness and Creativity," *Psychological Reports* 20 (1967), p. 822.

12. *Who's Who in America, 46th ed., Vol. I* (Wilmette, IL: Marquis, 1990), p. 1639.

13. Bruce M. Owen and Ronald Braeutigam, *The Regulation Game* (Cambridge: Ballinger Publishing, 1978), p. 9.

14. Lena Williams, "Companies Capitalizing on Worker Diversity," *New York Times,* December 15, 1992, pp. A1, D20.

15. David Jamieson and Julie O'Mara, *Managing Workforce 2000* (San Francisco: Jossey-Bass, 1991), p. 280; Taylor Cox, Jr., *Cultural Diversity in Organizations* (San Francisco: Berrett-Koehker, 1993), p. 313; Derald Wing Sue, "A Model for Cultural Diversity Training," *Journal of Counseling & Development,* September/October 1991, p. 105.

16. George R. Packard, "The U.S. and Japan: Partners in Prosperity," *Atlantic,* February 1989, p. A16.

17. Sidebar accompanying Walter Shapiro, "Is Washington in Japan's Pocket?" *Time,* October 1, 1990, p. 107.

18. *Washington Post,* October 8, 1989, p. C4.

19. George R. Packard, "Chrysanthemum and Sword," *New York Times,* March 8, 1993, p. A15.

20. Letter of June 8, 1993 from Leslie A. Cameron to author.

21. *Publication Manual of the American Psychological Association*, 3rd ed. (Washington, D.C.: American Psychological Association), sec. 3.85.

22. The Speech Communication Association's statement of authorship ethics timidly states that "acknowledgement of assistance, including that of graduate students, should be made" (see *The 1993 SCA Convention* [Annandale, VA: SCA, 1993], p. 243). The Association for Education in Journalism and Mass Communication (AEJMC), an academic organization devoted to enhancing the quality of newspapers and magazines, has no disclosure requirements for its journals. University of Texas professor James Tankard, the editor of one of the AEJMC's journals, reports that his journal "does not have stipulations or guidelines concerning conflicts of interest, funding received by professorial authors, or the like. We also do not have a published requirement that authors disclose outside funding for their research."

23. Jon Schamber and Michelle Ruffoni, "Assessing the Value of Consultants: 'How Do You Know if You've Done Good?'" Paper presented to the

1994 Convention of the Speech Communication Association, November 1994.

24. "A Comparison of the Effects of a Linear and an Exponential Performance Pay Function on Work Productivity," *Journal of Organizational Management Behavior,* Spring 1992, p. 85.

25. See *Communication Research,* July 1986, pp. 343-361; *Human Communication Research,* Summer 1989, pp. 493-508.

26. Typically, the salary estimated in a grant proposal is a fraction of the professor's salary. The money is enough to hire a part-time replacement but isn't sufficient to pay the grant recipient's actual salary.

27. *Journal of Broadcasting and Electronic Media,* Spring 1991, pp. 213-232, and Fall 1993, pp. 401-418.

28. April 1993, p. 387. The study examined the accuracy of putting in golf using a conventional putter and a 52-inch putter!

29. November/December 1992, p. 212. This study found that travellers obtain information about potential destinations from friends and family members.

30. Summer 1986, p. 495. This research "discovered" that speakers who look at their feet or at the ceiling while speaking aren't as effective as those who look at their audience.

31. Summer 1985, p. 1. This study examined whether newspapers' sales kits provide circulation or readership numbers.

32. Summer 1986, p. 389. This article reported that people get more cooking recipes from newspapers than television.

33. March 1992, p. 121. This study found that narcissists—people who pay inordinate attention to their appearance—are less satisfied with themselves than other people.

34. July/September 1992, p. 211. The article examined the relationship between hunting preferences, club membership, and media involvement among 277 goose hunters.

35. Select House Committee on Children, Youth and Families, 102nd Congress (2nd session), *College Education: Paying More and Getting Less* (Washington, D.C.: U.S. Government Printing Office, 1993), p. 4.

36. These estimates are based on listings in the Spring 1994 and Fall 1994-95 University of Wisconsin *Timetable.*

37. Tom Vanden Brook, "Share of Undergrad Classes Taught by Faculty Declines," *Milwaukee Journal,* September 2, 1994, p. 1.

38. Lawrence Soley, "With Whom Are Mass Communication Researchers Communicating?" Paper presented to the 1993 National Conference of the Association for Education in Journalism and Mass Communication, Kansas City, August 1993.

Notes to Chapter Six

1. *Company Fact Sheet* (Milwaukee: Johnson Controls, Inc., July 1993), p. 2. James Keyes is also a trustee of Marquette University.

2. The release was reprinted in part in "Company Will Provide UWM with $1 Million Design Grant," *Milwaukee Journal,* September 15, 1993, p. B3.

3. "The New York University Salomon Center," NYU Gopher File, accessible via Internet. "Applied academic research" is not conducted to generate theories or broaden understandings about how social institutions work. This is the purpose of "basic research." Applied research is designed specifically for use by firms or industries.

4. *New York University Salomon Center Newsletter,* Spring-Summer 1994, pp. 2-4.

5. "Oil and Gas Executive Commits $5 Million Gift to Business Education at SMU," Southwest Newswire, May 22, 1984. Maguire Oil is a Dallas-based company that produces crude petroleum and natural gas.

6. *Graduate Bulletin of Southern Methodist University* (Dallas: Southern Methodist University, 1992), pp. 101-102.

7. John Baden, "Crimes Against Nature: Public Funding of Environmental Destruction," *Policy Review,* Winter 1987, p. 36; Don Leal and John Baden, "Oil and Environmentalism Do Mix," *Chicago Tribune,* June 21, 1986, p. 9.

8. Don Leal and John Baden, "Oil and Environmentalism Do Mix," *ibid.* The embarrassing inaccuracy of Baden's assessment in the wake of the Exxon Valdez oil spill hasn't stopped him from continuing to trumpet the laurels of corporate environmentalism and the follies of government regulation. Baden has moved from SMU to the University of Washington, where he still chastises the government for trying to regulate corporate practices. For examples, see John A. Baden, "A Radical Proposal to Bail Out Smokey," *Seattle Times,* May 25, 1993, p. A11; John A. Baden, "America's Earth Day Supergift: Siberia," *Seattle Times,* April 20, 1994, p. B7; John A. Baden, "Free-Market Forces Favor Public Good, Not Privilege," *Seattle Times,* March 9, 1994, p. B7.

9. Stephen Pizzo, "Utah Officials Hit on T&Ls," *National Mortgage News,* March 23, 1992, p. 1.

10. Elaine B. Weis (ed.), *Restructuring the Financial System: Proceedings of the 1991 Annual Conference* (Salt Lake City: Garn Institute of Finance, February 7-9, 1991), p. 127.

11. Anne Lowrey Bailey, "Chrysler's Iacocca, Class of '45, Brings Verve to Lehigh U. Fund-raising Drive," *Chronicle of Higher Education,* December 2, 1987, pp. A1, A30-31.

12. "Worthy Cause?" *AutoWeek,* June 29, 1992, p. 10; Charles M. Thomas, "Chrysler Asks Dealers to Donate $1,000 for Tribute to Iacocca," *Automotive News,* June 15, 1992, p. 3.

13. "Iacocca Institute, Lehigh University, Mountaintop Dedication," promotional material dated June 6, 1991.

14. *Ibid.*

15. "Financial News," PR Newswire, August 31, 1992.

16. Ken Brown, "Fearing Shrunken Stature, France Endows a Fund," *New York Times,* February 23, 1994, p. B12.

17. *Messenger,* Report from the China Times Center for Media and Social Studies, August 1, 1990, p. 1.

18. Brenda Rotherham, "China to Offer Veneer of Reform, Scholar Says," *Minneapolis Star Tribune,* October 8, 1989, p. 13A. In May 1991, Taiwan's president Lee Teng-hui terminated the "Period of National Mobilization for the Suppression of the Communist Rebellion," which reduced the level of hostility between Taiwan and China.

19. "Saudi Gift Sets Up Islamic Law Center," *New York Times,* June 11, 1993, p. B8.

20. John B. Judis, "The Japanese Megaphone," *The New Republic* January 22, 1990, p. 22.

21. *Foundation Reporter 1992* (The Taft Group, 1992), p. 821; Karen Grassmuck, "Japanese Businessman's Background Stirs Debate over whether Colleges Should Accept His Gifts," *Chronicle of Higher Education,* May 2, 1990, p. 1.

22. *Foundation Reporter 1994,* 25th ed. (Washington, D.C.: The Taft Group, 1994), p. 1354.

23. Grassmuck, "Japanese Businessman's Background Stirs Debate," *op. cit.*

24. *Ibid.*

25. See John B. Judis, "A Yen for Approval," *Columbia Journalism Review,* January/February 1990, pp. 42-45; Pat Choate, *Agents of Influence* (New York: Alfred A. Knopf, 1990).

26. *Research Centers Directory, 7th ed.* (Detroit: Gale Research, 1982); *Research Centers Directory, 18th ed.* (Detroit: Gale Research, 1993).

27. *Ibid.,* p. 1143.

28. *Center for Mature Consumer Studies* (Atlanta: Georgia State University, undated promotional brochure); *Marketing to Older Consumers: A Handbook of Information for Strategy Development* (Westport, CT: Quorum Books, 1992), p. 1; "Use of Credit Cards by Older Americans," *Journal of Services Marketing,* Winter 1994, p. 27.

29. *Report of the State Auditor of Georgia, Personal Services and Travel Expense Supplement* (Atlanta: State of Georgia, 1993), p. 157.

30. *Research Center Directory, 18th ed.* (Detroit: Gale Research, 1993), p. 1144.

31. Michael I. Luger and Harvey A. Goldstein, *Technology in the Garden: Research Parks and Regional Economic Development* (Chapel Hill, University of North Carolina Press, 1991), p. 2.

32. Ellen T. Corliss, "Connecticut Incubator Parks Hatch Innovative Startups," *Mass High Tech*, November 6, 1989, p. 18.

33. Goldie Blumenstyk, "Pitfalls of Research Parks Lead Universities and States to Reassess Their Expectations," *Chronicle of Higher Education*, July 5, 1990, pp. A19, A24.

34. "Congress Funds Tech Park; Gives Grant to University of Connecticut for Projects, Including the Connecticut Technology Park," *American Machinist*, January 1993, p. 28.

35. Goldie Blumenstyk, "Pitfalls of Research Parks Lead Universities and States to Reassess Their Expectations," *op. cit.*

36. Thomas J. Chiconski (ed.), *Research Centers Directory* (Washington, D.C.: Gale Research, Inc., 1993), pp. 1752, 1787.

37. Michael I. Luger and Harvey A. Goldstein, *op. cit.*

Notes to Chapter Seven

1. Martin Anderson, *Impostors in the Temple* (New York: Simon & Schuster, 1992), p. 49.

2. Martin Anderson, "The Galls of Ivy: Our Professors Do Everything But Teach," *Washington Post*, October 18, 1992, p. C3.

3. For examples, see Martin Anderson, "How to Shrink the Deficit," *New York Times*, May 16, 1990, p. 27; Danica Kirka, "What Can Bill Clinton Do to Boost State Business?" *Los Angeles Times*, November 15, 1992, p. M1. When asked in a telephone interview about his own lack of teaching responsibilities at Stanford, Anderson replied that he is "at the Hoover Institution, a think tank which is an integral part of Stanford," and therefore is not required to teach. He offered the following explanation for his double standard in a telephone interview of June 27, 1994: "I have taught courses at Columbia, where I had tenure."

4. *Hoover Institution Report 1990* (Stanford, CA: Stanford University, 1990), p. 32.

5. Allan Bloom, *The Closing of the American Mind* (New York: Simon and Schuster, 1987), p. 321.

6. Many other right-wing university critics also avoid stepping into the classroom. For example, Herbert London, a co-founder of the National Association of Scholars, the organization that functions as an anecdote bank about incidents of "political correctness," was dean rather than a teacher at the Gallatin Division of New York University. Instead of lecturing, grading, or advising students, London served as a fellow at the Hudson Institute and the Ethics and Public Policy Center, two off-campus think tanks; was a member of the advisory board of the Center for the Study of Political and Social Change, a conservative think tank at Smith College;

ran for governor of New York as the Conservative Party candidate during 1989; and in 1993 was the Republican Party candidate for New York State Comptroller. One of London's associates at the Gallatin Division said that he hadn't taught a course there in ten years.

7. *Center for Study of Public Choice, Annual Report 1990* (Fairfax, VA: George Mason University, 1991), p. 1.

8. Quoted in James A. Smith, *The Idea Brokers* (New York: The Free Press, 1991), p. 186.

9. *Hoover Institution Report 1990, op. cit.* All subsequent discussions of the Hoover Institution concern staff and fellows present during the 1989-90 academic year.

10. The John M. Olin Foundation is one of six conservative foundations that collectively have assets of about $925 million and pour about $40 million annually into conservative on- and off-campus think tanks, many of which promote the idea that political correctness, rather than corporate influence, is rampant on college campuses. The other foundations that fund the think tanks are the Sarah Scaife, Smith Richardson, J. M., Earhart, and Lynde and Harry Bradley foundations.

11. Hoover fellows are also interbred with many other university-based think tanks. Hoover fellows are associated with the University of Chicago's Center for the Study of the Economy and the State, Smith College's Center for the Study of Social and Political Change in Northampton, and Southwest Missouri State University's Center for Defense and Strategic Studies.

12. *The Center for International Security and Strategic Studies Annual Report 1990* (Mississippi State, MS: Mississippi State University, 1991), p. 2.

13. Amy Wilentz, "On the Intellectual Ramparts," *Time*, September 1, 1986, pp. 1, 22-23.

14. "All the Usual Suspects: 'MacNeil/Lehrer' and 'Nightline,'" *Extra!* Winter 1990, pp. 1-11.

15. *Ibid.*

16. However, most conservatives classify the AEI as on the right. For example, see Gregory Wolfe, *Right Minds* (Washington, D.C.: 1988), p. 208; and Roger Meiners and David Leband, *Patterns of Corporate Philanthropy* (Washington, D.C.: Capital Research Center, 1988), p. 327.

17. *American Enterprise Annual Report 1988-1989* (Washington, D.C.: American Enterprise Institute, 1990), p. 31.

18. *Heritage Foundation Annual Report 1988* (Washington, D.C.: Heritage Foundation, 1989).

19. Gregg Easterbrook, "Ideas Move Nations," *Atlantic Monthly,* January 1986, pp. 66-80; Peter Stone, "Businesses Widen Role in Conservative 'War of Ideas,'" *Washington Post,* May 12, 1985, pp. F3-F5.

20. Alison Muscatine, "Georgetown University and its Media Stars," *Washington Post National Weekly Edition,* May 26, 1986, pp. 10-11.

21. *New York Times,* November 28, 1987, p. 46.

22. *1988 Annual Report* (Washington, D.C.: Cato Institute, 1989), p. 27.

23. Jim Mann, "Taiwan a Big Contributor to Think Tanks," *Los Angeles Times,* September 5, 1988, p. 10.

24. *American Enterprise Annual Report 1988-1989, op. cit.*

25. Ellen Frankel Paul, "Bared Buttocks and Federal Cases," *Society,* May/June 1991, p. 6.

26. Ellen Frankel Paul, "Forbidden Grounds: The Case Against Employment Discrimination Laws" (review), *The Cato Journal,* Winter 1993, p. 741.

27. *IHS The Institute for Humane Studies 1990 Annual Report* (Fairfax, VA: George Mason University, 1991), pp. 16, 19.

28. Institute for Humane Studies, *1990 Annual Report* (Fairfax, VA: George Mason University, 1990), p. 1.

29. *John M. Olin Institute for Strategic Studies, Annual Report 1991-1992* (Cambridge, MA: Harvard University's Center for International Affairs, 1992), p. 33.

30. *Hoover Institution Report 1990, op. cit.,* p. 32.

31. *The Center for International Affairs Annual Report 1991-1992* (Cambridge, MA: Harvard University, 1992), p. 12.

32. *Fellowship Information* (Fairfax, VA: Institute for Humane Studies, 1990).

33. Judith Cummings, "Hispanic People Gaining in New Jobs," *New York Times,* April 2, 1987, p. A26.

34. Edwin J. Feulner, "The Stake in the Economy's Heart," *Chief Executive,* November 1992, p. 14.

35. *Annual Report July 1, 1987 - June 1, 1988* (New York: Council on Foreign Relations, 1988), p. 167.

36. Robert F. Nagel and Jack H. Nagel, "Theory of Choice," *The New Republic,* July 23, 1990, p. 15.

37. Bradley Policy Research Center, *Annual Report 1990-1991* (Rochester: University of Rochester, 1991), p. 4.

38. *The Center for National Security Law: Report on the First Decade* (Charlottesville, VA: University of Virginia, 1992), pp. 2, 62-63.

39. *Ibid.,* p. 64.

40. *Report of Operations 1990* (Cambridge, MA: Institute for Foreign Policy Analysis, 1991), p. 7.

41. See Robert L. Pfaltzgraff, Jr., "An Unjustly Criticized Patriot," *Wall Street Journal,* April 8, 1992, p. A20; *Study War No More* (Cambridge, MA: University Conversion Project, 1994), pp. 32-34.

42. "Councils of Caution Undercut Peace in Gulf," *Christian Science Monitor,* December 3, 1990, p. 19; "Killing Saddam: Would It Be a Crime?" *Washington Post,* October 7, 1990, p. D1.

43. See *Houston Chronicle,* December 22, 1991, p. B1, and March 23, 1993, p. A13.

44. "The Use of Soviet Scientists, Scholars and Educators for Propaganda and Disinformation," *Propaganda Disinformation Persuasion,* Spring 1991, p. 105.

45. Alexander is now at George Washington University, where he oversees a terrorism project.

46. For explanations concerning the repeated use of these "experts," see Edward Herman and Noam Chomsky, *Manufacturing Consent* (New York: Pantheon, 1988); and Edward Herman and Gerry O'Sullivan, *The "Terrorism" Industry* (New York: Pantheon, 1989).

Notes to Chapter Eight

1. For a discussion of the appeal to vanity, see Kathleen Teltsch, "For a Price, Immortality on Campus," *New York Times,* June 11, 1993, p. A14.

2. From the Chair, Senate, "Documents Relating to the Endowment of the Reliance Professorship/Deanship," *Almanac,* January 27, 1981, p. 3. As a result of faculty protests at Penn, the wording of the agreement between Steinberg and the university was eventually changed.

3. "Philanthropy Notes," *Chronicle of Higher Education,* May 12, 1993, p. A38.

4. "Federal Jury Convicts 2 Officers of a Failed Austin, Texas, Thrift," *Wall Street Journal,* October 25, 1991, p. 2.

5. William Bentinck-Smith and Elizabeth Stouffer, *Harvard University History of Endowed Chairs* (Cambridge: Harvard's Office of the University Publisher, 1991); "Philanthropy Notes," *Chronicle of Higher Education,* December 16, 1992, p. A28.

6. Mike Kaszuba, "Critics Say Gift Influenced 'U' Choice of Travel Agency," *Minneapolis Star Tribune,* July 9, 1990, p. 3B.

7. Maura Lerner, "Endowed Chair for Tourism at 'U' May Be a First," *Minneapolis Star Tribune,* February 28, 1991, p. B3.

8. *University of California Academic Salary Scales* (Oakland: Office of the President, July 1991).

9. UCLA's *Schedule of Classes* for the Fall 1993, Winter 1994, and Spring 1994 terms; correspondence of March 29, 1995.

10. *Who's Who in America 1995, 49th ed.* (New Providence, NJ: Marquis Who's Who, 1994), pp. 2871-2872.

11. Dorothy Clifford, "The James Madison Institute: Tallahassee's Think Tank," *Tallahassee Democrat,* September 27, 1989, p. 1D, 3D; Tom Oberhafer, "Income Tax Talk is Government Ploy to Spend More," *St. Petersburg Times,* July 30, 1991, p. 2. The president of the James Madison Institute is a former Florida State University president.

12. *Endowment Funding Guidelines* (revised 1/24/86) (Baltimore: Johns Hopkins University, 1986).

13. "Duke University Endowment Minimums" and "Duke University Distinguished Professorships," Duke University News Service, 1992.

14. *Facts—the University of Texas at Austin 1991* (Austin: University of Texas, 1991), p. 6.

15. William Bentinck-Smith and Elizabeth Stouffer, *Harvard History of Named Chairs, op. cit.,* p. 7.

16. Susan Heller Anderson, "Chronicle," *New York Times,* June 16, 1991, p. B10.

17. Samantha Conti, "Professor by Fiat," *Lingua Franca,* June/July 1992, pp. 5-6.

18. *Ibid.*; Howard Kurz, "Fiat Connection Rocks Top Journalism School," *Houston Chronicle,* July 5, 1992, p. A23.

19. Anthony Shugaar, "A Columbia Professor by His own Fiat, Agnelli's Man in N.Y. Wears Out Welcome," *New York Observer,* July 19-26, 1993, pp. 1, 17.

20. *Ibid.*, p. 17.

21. John B. Judis, "The Japanese Megaphone," *The New Republic,* January 22, 1990, p. 22.

22. Leslie Helm, "On Campus: Fat Cat Endowments and Growing Clout," *Business Week,* July 11, 1988, pp. 70-71.

23. Jean Evangelauf, "Fearing Colleges Slight 'Traditional Values,' Conservatives Back 'Free Enterprise' Chairs," *Chronicle of Higher Education,* June 24, 1987, pp. 10-12.

24. Telephone interview of February 14, 1992.

25. Martin Morse Wooster, "Chairs of Entrepreneurship Are Bad Business," *Wall Street Journal,* May 5, 1990, p. A16.

26. "The Yankee Institute and Shelby Cullom Davis Endowment Sponsor the First New England Education Summit," PR Newswire, October 5, 1988. The symposium featured high-profile rightists and think-tank denizens such as former U.S. assistant secretary of education Chester E. Finn, Dennis Doyle of the Hudson Institute, Robert Woodson of the National Center for Neighborhood Enterprise, and John Chubb of the Brookings Institution.

27. "News Advisory on Steinberg Memorial Lecture," PR Newswire, April 10, 1989; "U.S. Secretary of Defense Dick Cheney to Speak at Wharton, November 5," U.S. Newswire, October 30, 1991.

28. Chris Welles, "Fit or Unfit Business News," in William McPhatter (ed.), *The Business Beat: Its Impact & Its Problems* (Indianapolis: Bobbs-Merrill, 1980), pp. 33-34.

29. Carol Schwartz and Rebecca Turner, *Encyclopedia of Associations, 29th ed.* (Detroit: Gale Research, 1994) p. 2011.

30. Dwight R. Lee, "Mandated Benefits; The Cost of President Clinton's Proposed Worker Benefits," *Society,* May 1994, p. 14.

31. See Lawrence C. Soley, "Pundits in Print," *Newspaper Research Journal,* Spring 1994, pp. 65-75, which discusses how professorial titles at-

tract the attention of reporters. The more impressive the title, the more likely it is that a professor will be quoted as an "expert."

32. *Constitutional Economics: Containing the Economic Powers of Government*, although described on the jacket as "A Heritage Foundation Book," was published by Lexington Books. The book, a collection of papers from a Heritage Foundation conference, was edited rather than written by McKenzie.

33. William E. Simon, "Preface," in Roger E. Meiners and David N. Laband, *Patterns of Corporate Philanthropy* (Washington, D.C.: Capital Research Center, 1988), pp. v-vi.

34. In *The Politics of Rich and Poor* (New York; Random House, 1990), p. 65, Kevin Phillips, a Republican critic of the ultraright, describes the Law and Economics movement as a neo-Darwinist "theology" reminiscent of the views of Herbert Spencer and William Graham Sumner. According to Phillips, Law and Economics theology preaches that "commercial selection processes in the marketplace could largely displace government decision-making. One intellectual frontiersman, Richard Posner, University of Chicago law professor turned federal appeals court judge…suggested making a market for babies so that it would be easier for couples to adopt. A second prominent Chicago legalist, Richard A. Epstein, leader of the movement's 'economic rights' faction, deplored most government economics regulation as unconstitutional." Phillips contends that the Law and Economics movement was a fringe ideology before Reagan's inauguration, but has since moved into the mainstream.

35. D'Vera Cohn, "New Dean Brings Upheaval to Mason Law School," *Washington Post,* November 4, 1987, p. B1; "Mason Builds," *Legal Times,* June 1, 1987, p. 3.

36. Loren Feldman, "Tracking to the Right at George Mason," *op. cit.*

37. Jay Mathews, "Business Tries to Shape Legal System, Report Says," *Washington Post,* May 19, 1993, p. F4.

38. As stated on National Public Radio's "Morning Edition," May 24, 1993.

39. *Ibid.*

40. Jon Weiner, "Dollars for Neocon Scholars," *Nation,* January 1, 1990, pp. 12-13.

41. Alliance for Justice, *Justice for Sale* (Washington, D.C.: Alliance for Justice, 1993), p. 37.

42. *Ibid.*, pp. 31-33.

43. John M. Olin Program in Law and Economics, *1989-90 Annual Report* (Stanford, CA: Stanford Law School, undated).

44. Nan Aron, Barbara Moulten, and Chris Owens, "Economics, Academia, and Corporate Money in America: The 'Law and Economics' Movement," *Antitrust and Economic Review*, 1993, pp. 27-42.

45. Chris Welles, *op. cit.*, p. 34.

46. Ronald Alsop, "Capitalism 101: Programs to Teach Free Enterprise Sprout on College Campuses," *Wall Street Journal,* May 10, 1978, p. 37.

47. Timothy Mescon, dean of Kennesaw's business school, claims that he recruited Gingrich to teach the class. Mescon's father, Michael, was a former dean and free enterprise chair holder at Georgia State, before retiring to set up the Mescon Group, a consulting firm with ties to Gingrich (see Doug Cumming, "Newt Gingrich at Kennesaw State," *Atlanta Journal and Constitution,* September 19, 1993, p. F8). Kennesaw's business school also houses the Georgia-Cobb Free Enterprise Chair.

48. Charles Walston, "Gingrich College Class Raises Questions," *Atlanta Journal and Constitution,* September 2, 1993, p. A1.

49. Robert Vickers, "Gingrich Moves Course to Reinhardt College," *Atlanta Journal and Constitution,* November 6, 1993, p. B10; Stephen Engelberg and Katharine Seelye, "Gingrich: Man in Spotlight and Organization in Shadow," *New York Times,* December 18, 1994, pp. A1, A20.

Notes to Chapter Nine

1. Telephone interview of June 7, 1993.

2. One of the articles that this professor wrote appeared in an APA-affiliated publication.

3. Most statistics in this chapter are from the university self-reports published in American Council on Education, *American Universities and Colleges, 14th ed.* (New York: Walter de Gruyter, 1992). The 1980 data came from the 12th edition of this publication. The University of Michigan statistics are from "UM Research Outlays at an All-time High," *Michigan Today,* March 1995, p. 6. Just as tuition has helped pay for university research, patient fees at academic hospitals have been used to subsidize research. Many academic hospitals admit this, but deny that their research spending has contributed to the increased costs of medical care. For a discussion of patient subsidies to medical research, see Elisabeth Rosenthal, "Elite Hospitals in New York City Are Facing a Major Crunch," *New York Times,* February 13, 1995, p. A13.

4. William Celis III, "The Big Stars on Campus Are Now Research Labs," *New York Times,* December 4, 1994, pp. 1, 18.

5. Tom Vanden Brook, "UWM Meets Mandate to Cut $1.85 Million," *Milwaukee Journal,* December 30, 1994, p. B1.

6. The increase in expenditures reported in the table is not as great as it seems. Although it appears that the 1991 education expenditure of $229.2 million was more than double the expenditure in 1980, it wasn't, when adjusted for Consumer Price Index (CPI) increases. In 1991, the university would have needed to spend $175 million on instruction just to keep instructional spending even with 1980 levels.

7. Don Horine, "Professors Teach Less than 12 Hours a Week," *Palm Beach Post*, January 18, 1995, p. 1A.

8. *Research Centers Directory, 18th ed.* (Washington, D.C.: Gale Research, 1994), p. 1772.

9. This doesn't simply mean that high school dropouts should be appointed as trustees, but that social workers, psychologists, educators, and others who can address the needs of the poor and disadvantaged—and can represent them—should be. The same can be said for other constituencies.

 Index

A

ABC. *See* American Broadcasting Company
ACE Denken Company, 7, 164n19
Administration. *See* College executive officers (CEOs)
Advertisement, corporate
from donations, 6-7
of tobacco companies, 58-61
See also Media
AEI. *See* American Enterprise Institute
African Americans, 7
and political correctness, 1, 3, 4
and tuition, 11
American Broadcasting Company (ABC), 84
American Enterprise Institute (AEI), 73, 109, 111, 112, 113-14
and political correctness, 5, 6, 14
See also Think tanks
American Psychological Association (APA), 82-83
Anderson, Martin, 3, 6, 107-8, 182n3
APA. *See* American Psychological Association
Association of Private Enterprise Education, 134-36
Athletics, 31-33
AT&T, 64-65

B

Bach, Fitz, 43
Baden, John, 93-94, 180n8
Bagdikian, Ben, 20
Balch, Stephen, 2, 6, 20-21
Bass, Edward, 13-14
Beecham Group Pharmaceuticals, 47-48

Betrayers of Truth (Broad/Wade), 53
Biomedical research. *See* Medical research
Biosphere 2, 13-14, 165n40
Blackwell, Roger, 61
Bluestone, Charles, 47-48
Bocca, Giorgio, 131
Boren, David, 19-20
Boston University (BU), 6, 21-24
Bowling Green State University, 110, 115
Bradford, Cal, 7
Braeutigam, Ronald, 80
Braude, Abraham, 46
Breuning, Stephen, 51
Bristol-Meyers, 9
Broad, Eli, 70-71
Broad, William, 53
Brookings Institution, 80. *See also* Think tanks
BU. *See* Boston University
Burbank, Alice, 125
Buresh, Bernice, 22
Business school
and corporate consultation, 57-65
and corporate ties, 57-61
individual donations to, 70-71
journals, 62, 65-67
research centers, 71-74
salaries, 62-63
teaching requirements, 66-70
tuition, 69-70

C

Cantekin, Erden, 47-48
Capitalism, 11. *See also* Endowed professorships; Think tanks
Carey, James, 2
Carlson, Curt, 127

About South End Press

South End Press is a non-profit, collectively run book publisher with over 180 titles in print. Since our founding in 1977, we have tried to meet the needs of readers who are exploring, or are already committed to, the politics of radical social change.

Our goal is to publish books that encourage critical thinking and constructive action on the key political, cultural, social, economic, and ecological issues shaping life in the United States and in the world. In this way, we hope to give expression to a wide diversity of democratic social movements and to provide an alternative to the products of corporate publishing.

Through the Institute for Social and Cultural Change, South End Press works with other political media project—Z Magazine, Speak Out! a speakers bureau; and the Publishers Support Project—to expand access to information and critical analysis. If you would like a free catalog of South End Press books or information about our membership program, which offers two free books and a 40 percent discount on all titles, please write to us at: South End Press, 116 Saint Botolph Street, Boston, MA 02115.

Other South End Press Titles of Interest

Too Close for Comfort: The Fascist Potential of the U.S. Right,
by Chip Berlet and Matthew Lyons

Networks of Power: Corporate TV's Threat to Democracy,
by Dennis W. Mazzocco

CIA Off Campus
by Ami Chen Mills

New Voices: Student Political Activism in the '80s and '90s
by Tony Vellela

About the Author

Lawrence C. Soley is the Colnik Professor of Communication at Marquette University in Milwaukee. He previously taught at the University of Minnesota, University of Georgia, the Pennsylvania State University, and the City University of New York. His previous books include *The News Shapers, Radio Warfare,* and *Clandestine Radio Broadcasting* (with J. Nichols), which was selected as one of the "outstanding" books of 1987 by *Choice* magazine. His investigative reporting and research has won the prestigious Sigma Delta Chi Award and the American Academy of Advertising's "Best Article Award."